# workskills™
## Math

**PROGRAM CONSULTANTS**

Bonnie Goonen

Susan Pittman-Shetler

Steck-Vaughn®

HOUGHTON MIFFLIN HARCOURT

www.steckvaughn.com/adulted
800-289-4490

Photo Acknowledgements:
P. cover ©Corbis; 4 (bl), 22–23, 60–61 ©moodboard/Getty Images; 4 (c), 82–83 ©Pamela Moore/Getty Images; 4 (tl), 112–113 ©Noel Hendrickson/Getty Images; 5 ©Siede Preis/Photodisc/Getty Images.

Printed in the U.S.A.

ISBN   978-0-547-53645-3

3 4 5 6 7 8 9 10   1689   20 19 18 17 16 15 14 13 12 11

4500305961        A B C D E F G

# Table of Contents

Welcome to Steck-Vaughn's *WorkSkills*™     4

Review of Basic Skills     12

Pretest Assessment (online)     🖱

**Chapter 1   Problem Solving**

Lesson 1: Get Started with Problem Solving     24

Lesson 2: Identify What Information Is Needed     32

Lesson 3: Use Strategies to Problem Solve     40

Lesson 4: Solve the Problem     48

Skills for the Workplace: Determine the Reasonableness of an Answer     56

Chapter 1 Assessment 🖱     58

**Chapter 2   Number Operations**

Lesson 5: Work with Currency     62

Lesson 6: Understand Percents     70

Skills for the Workplace: Make Correct Change     78

Chapter 2 Assessment 🖱     80

**Chapter 3   Measurement and Geometry**

Lesson 7: Measurement on the Job     84

Lesson 8: Conversions     92

Lesson 9: Formulas     100

Skills for the Workplace: Precision—Rounding     108

Chapter 3 Assessment 🖱     110

**Chapter 4   Data**

Lesson 10: Compute Data     114

Lesson 11: Interpret Charts and Tables     122

Lesson 12: Compare and Contrast Data     130

Skills for the Workplace: Create a Table     138

Chapter 4 Assessment 🖱     140

OFFICIAL Work Readiness Practice Test (online)     🖱

*WorkSkills*™ Glossary     142

Answers and Solutions     144

🖱 = Online Assessments

# Welcome to Steck-Vaughn's *WorkSkills*™

## Setting Yourself Apart in Today's Job Market

You probably already know that finding the right job for you can be a time-consuming and sometimes difficult process. You may have to sort through hundreds of job listings in order to find the few that seem right for your skills and experience.

The same is true for employers. A manager may receive hundreds or even thousands of applications for only a few open positions. How can you make yourself stand out as one of the best applicants for the job?

When looking for entry-level workers, employers want to be assured that a new employee has the knowledge and skills that he or she needs in order to be successful. Many of the skills that can help you stand out to a potential employer are also skills that you use every day. Have you ever:

- read or written an e-mail?

- estimated whether you had enough money to buy something?

- resolved a conflict with a friend or family member?

- spoken with a technical support person to solve a problem with your cell phone or computer?

If so, then you have used skills that employers value and that will help you succeed in finding and keeping a job.

**Steck-Vaughn's *WorkSkills*™** is designed to assist you in identifying these skills and **developing your strengths** in these areas. Together with the **National Work Readiness Credential**, *WorkSkills*™ helps you prove to potential employers that **you are ready for a great career!**

# What Can the National Work Readiness Credential Do for You?

Some skills are specific to a particular job. If you work in construction, you probably don't need to know how to operate a cash register. However, there are other skills that apply to almost every job. The National Work Readiness Council has worked with employers in many fields to identify the knowledge, skills, and abilities needed by entry-level employees. These skills fall into four main categories:

- **Communication Skills:** reading with understanding, listening actively, speaking clearly, and thinking critically

- **Interpersonal Skills:** cooperating with others, negotiating, resolving conflicts, and giving and receiving support

- **Decision-Making Skills:** identifying and solving problems (including some that require math), making decisions, and planning ahead

- **Lifelong Learning Skills:** taking responsibility for your own learning, identifying your strengths and weaknesses, and being willing and motivated to learn new skills

Earning the National Work Readiness Credential shows employers that you have these skills. It also shows that you are motivated, have a strong work ethic, and are willing to take initiative. These qualities will set you apart from many other people who are applying for the same jobs that you are. The National Work Readiness Credential gives you an edge by showing employers that you have what it takes to succeed on the job.

To earn the National Work Readiness Credential, you will need to take and pass four separate tests:

- **Reading**

- **Math**

- **Situational Judgment**

- **Active Listening**

## Prove Your Potential with *WorkSkills*™

The *WorkSkills*™ series is designed to provide you with the instruction and practice you need to master the National Work Readiness Credential assessment. This series will help you make progress toward your career goals. The *WorkSkills*™ books focus on applying reading, math, listening and speaking, and interpersonal skills in real-world workplace scenarios. In these books, all of the skills and strategies you learn will be taught in the context of real workplace scenarios, the kinds of situations that you will encounter on the job. Each lesson will teach the strategy, show you how to apply it, and then give you lots of examples that allow you to practice applying the skill or strategy to real workplace situations.

### Consistent Lesson Structure Enhances Mastery

Every lesson in the *WorkSkills*™ series uses the same format. This uniform structure enables you to gradually master each skill.

### Build on What You Know

This section introduces the skills by making connections to your daily life or in the workplace. The Essential Skills that you will be learning are clearly identified on the first page of the lesson. The "In Real Life" features connect and apply these skills to workplace scenarios.

### Develop Your Skills

This section provides in-depth instruction on the skills or strategies that are the focus of the lesson. Examples illustrate how to apply skills and strategies in workplace situations, and questions guide you through the steps you will use to successfully apply these strategies on your own. The "Got It?" feature summarizes the key points you should remember from each lesson.

### Apply Your Knowledge

Practice with the skills and strategies you have learned. A "To Do List" gives you a reminder of key points and processes, while another "In Real Life" scenario provides an opportunity to take what you have learned and apply it to another workplace scenario. "Think About It!" gives you a chance to reflect on what you have learned and the different ways that you can use it in the workplace.

### Test Your WRC Skills

Each lesson concludes with a *Test Your WRC Skills* section. These pages use questions modeled after those you will see on the National Work Readiness Credential assessment to give you practice applying the skills you have learned. Answers are provided at the back of the book.

## Assessments

The *WorkSkills*™ series includes a number of tools to help you assess what you already know, identify the skill areas on which you may need to focus, and monitor your progress as you study. In addition, there are several other opportunities, both within the books and online, for you to practice applying your skills by answering questions that are similar to those you will see on the National Work Readiness Credential assessment.

## Review of Basic Skills

The *WorkSkills*™ Math book includes a chapter that allows you to review basic math skills, such as operations with whole numbers, decimals, and fractions, as well as ratios, percents, and basic geometric shapes. Use this chapter to assess whether you need to solidify your foundational math skills before beginning your *WorkSkills*™ Math studies.

## Online Pretests

Before you begin your studies in this book, take the Online Pretest, which is a full-length practice version of the National Work Readiness Credential assessment. The questions on the Pretest mimic those on the National Work Readiness Credential assessment.

## Chapter Assessments
### Student Book Chapter Assessments

At the end of each chapter in the book, questions similar to those on the National Work Readiness Credential assessment allow you to determine whether you have mastered the Essential Skills that you learned in the chapter.

### Additional Online Chapter Assessments

The Online Chapter Assessments allow you to evaluate your mastery of the skills taught in the chapter you have just completed, as well as skills taught in previous chapters of the book. The questions are similar in style to those you will see on the National Work Readiness Credential assessment.

## Online OFFICIAL Work Readiness Practice Tests

The Online OFFICIAL Work Readiness Practice Tests are the full-length practice version of the National Work Readiness Credential assessment and are endorsed by the National Work Readiness Council. Use your results to assess what you have learned and where additional study may be needed.

## Answers and Solutions

You can quickly check your answers for each student book Chapter Assessment question, as well as the *Test Your WRC Skills* sections, in the *Answers and Solutions* section in the back of the book. This feature provides the correct answer, as well as a full explanation for why each answer choice is correct or incorrect. When taking the Online Chapter Assessments, you will get automated feedback.

# The National Work Readiness Credential

Today's adult education and workforce development programs face significant challenges in adequately preparing adults for entry into the workplace. However, the National Work Readiness Council has issued a new credential based on the *Equipped for the Future* standards. According to the NWRC, the new National Work Readiness Credential assessment assists educational professionals in:

- Assessing a learner's skills and needs.

- Creating learning experiences based on a simple standard of integrated skills and tasks.

- Providing competency goals that are useful for instruction and aspirational for learners.

- Aligning instruction to a standard defined by business.

- Demonstrating performance outcomes to funding organizations.

> " Getting and keeping a job is an important first step to meeting the demands of adulthood and self-sufficiency. "
>
> —Joe Mizereck,
> Acting Executive Director of the
> National Work Readiness Council

The National Work Readiness Credential assessment is designed to assess a worker's on-the-job skills in four areas: reading, math, situational judgment, and active listening.

## Steck-Vaughn's *WorkSkills*™ Series

If adult education and workforce development programs are to prepare students to pass the National Work Readiness Credential assessment, they need material that assists them in making the connection between what they learn in the classroom and how they can use that information in the workplace. Steck-Vaughn's *WorkSkills*™ series is designed to prepare adult learners to successfully pass the National Work Readiness Credential assessment and earn the National Work Readiness Credential. The series has been designed to cover all Domains and Essential Tasks, as identified by the National Work Readiness Council. Mastery of these tasks is viewed as necessary for adults to effectively be prepared for entry-level positions.

**Steck-Vaughn's *WorkSkills*™ is endorsed by the**

## Benefits That Set *WorkSkills*™ Apart

- Contextualized and integrated instruction
- Focus on real-world, workplace contexts and skills
- Gradual-release model of modeling-practice-application-test
- Written for non-traditional learners: approachable tone and accessible format
- Controlled readability, ranging from 7.0–8.9
- Print, online, and audio components
- Assessments that mimic the actual National Work Readiness Credential assessment:
  - Online Pretests
  - Online OFFICIAL Work Readiness Practice Tests
  - Chapter Assessments (available in print and online)
  - *Test Your WRC Skills* sections
- Answer keys with explanations/solutions
- Workplace Glossary

## Components of the *WorkSkills*™ series include:

### Available in Print

*WorkSkills*™ Reading

*WorkSkills*™ Math

*WorkSkills*™ Situational Judgment and Active Listening

### Available Online

- Online Pretests
- Downloadable Scenarios/Audio Scripts for Active Listening
- Additional Chapter Assessment questions

- Online OFFICIAL Work Readiness Practice Tests
- Online Teacher Lessons, available as printable PDFs

**For online assessments and instructor support, visit www.mysteckvaughn.com/WORK.**

# Steck-Vaughn's *WorkSkills*™ Math

All three books in the *WorkSkills*™ series have been designed to address the Work Readiness Domains and Essential Tasks. The *WorkSkills*™ Math book first focuses on problem-solving skills, applicable to all areas of math, and then emphasizes those skills in chapters that cover other math content. Essential Tasks are the focus for each lesson.

I. Problem Solving
II. Number Operations
III. Measurement and Geometry
IV. Data

## Math Skills and Problem-Solving Strategies for the Workplace

This book teaches students the skills and strategies needed to successfully solve problems on the job, models how to use them to solve workplace problems, and then gives numerous examples so students can practice in the context of workplace situations. Skills and strategies include:

- Develop and apply problem-solving strategies
- Use estimation to determine the reasonableness of answers
- Work with money, including making change and handling budgets
- Use appropriate measures, measurement units, and measurement tools
- Work with data and graphical displays of data, such as tables and charts

## Real-World Workplace Scenarios

Mathematics and problem-solving skills are integral to every job in some way. Therefore, the National Work Readiness Credential assessment presents realistic problems from the workplace. To provide ample opportunities to build the skills necessary to use math and problem-solving skills on the job, *WorkSkills*™ Math includes a heavy emphasis on teaching and practicing the strategies and skills using a variety of real-world workplace situations.

# Workforce Readiness
## Real World. Real Skills.

## ■ The *WorkSkills*™ Math Lesson at a Glance

**Essential Tasks**

Each chapter focuses on Essential Tasks within multiple domains, providing a foundation for problem solving and subsequently building on that while integrating new skills. The lessons within a chapter emphasize this integral approach by focusing on the Essential Tasks critical to workplace skills, which often pull from multiple domains.

**Online Teacher Lessons**

The online teacher lessons, available as printable PDFs, provide instructors with strategies and activities to help students master math skills and problem-solving strategies.

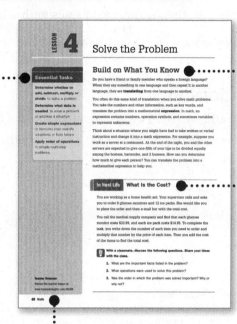

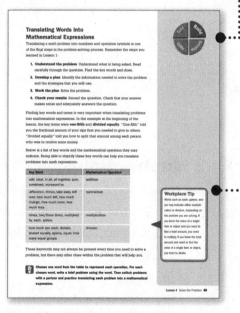

**Controlled Readability**

The readability of instruction is controlled, averaging between 7.0–8.9.

**Real-World Workplace Scenarios**

Students practice applying math skills and strategies in the context of workplace scenarios.

**Four-Step Process**

The gradual-release model of instruction enables learners to Build, Develop, and Apply new skills. Then learners Test their skills to assess their understanding.

**Workplace Tip**

These examples and helpful tips enable students to apply what they learn in the lesson to the workplace.

## Purchase the
## National Work Readiness Credential assessment

Steck-Vaughn has proudly partnered with the National Work Readiness Council to be the exclusive distributor of the National Work Readiness Credential assessment. Contact your sales representative for more details. You may also contact our customer service team at **800-289-4490** or visit our website at **www.steckvaughn.com/adulted**.

# Review of Basic Skills

In the workplace you need to have mastery of basic addition, subtraction, multiplication, and division skills with whole numbers, decimals, and fractions.

Let's review each math skill!

## Addition

To add two or more whole numbers, you need to:

- Add from right to left, starting with the ones column.
- Carry as necessary.

**Examples:**

```
                    1              1 1
    4            312            1,342
  + 6          + 168          +    69
  ----          -----          ------
   10            480           1,411
```

**It's Your Turn!**

```
1.    56        2.    29        3.    942
    + 17            + 48            + 678
    ----            ----            -----


4.    64        5.    212       6.    660
     520             311              61
    + 50             203             382
    ----           + 62            + 17
                   ----            -----
```

## Subtraction

To subtract two or more whole numbers you need to:

- Put the greater number on top.
- Subtract from right to left, starting with the ones column.
- Borrow as necessary.

**Examples:**

```
                                      13
                    6 13          2 14 12
    9              7 3            3 4 2
  - 4            - 17            -168
  ---             ---            -----
    5              56             174
```

**It's Your Turn!**

```
1.    46        2.    73        3.    61
    - 27            -  6            - 33
    ----            ----            ----


4.    33        5.    610       6.  4,864
    - 11            - 23          - 1,602
    ----            ----          -------
```

# Multiplication

To multiply a one-digit whole number by another whole number, you need to:

- Multiply from right to left, starting with the ones column.
- Carry as necessary.

**Examples:**

```
                  7 3            2 2 1
     4            194            1,342
  ×  6          ×   8          ×     7
  ────          ─────          ───────
    24          1,552            9,394
```

## It's Your Turn!

```
 1.    36         2.    29         3.   132
    ×   2            ×    8           ×    9
    ─────            ──────           ──────
```

```
 4.   129         5.   1,056        6.   2,694
    ×    8           ×      5           ×      3
    ──────           ─────────          ─────────
```

To multiply multi-digit whole numbers, you need to:

- Multiply each digit in the top factor by each digit in the bottom factor.
- Add the products together.

**Examples:**

```
                                   2,308
    14            334            ×   144
  × 16          ×  28            ───────
  ────          ──────            9,232
    84          2,672            92,320
   140          6,680           230,800
  ────          ──────          ───────
   224          9,352           332,352
```

## It's Your Turn!

```
 7.    56         8.    92         9.   152
    ×  12            ×  48            ×   57
    ─────            ──────           ──────
```

```
10.   206        11.   494        12.   335
   ×   37           ×  221           × 857
   ──────           ──────           ──────
```

# Division

To divide a whole number by another whole number, you need to:

- Divide from left to right.
- Determine how many times the divisor can go into each place in the dividend. Write that number in the quotient.
- Multiply that number by the divisor. Write the product below the appropriate place in the dividend, and subtract.
- Bring down the number in the next place. Repeat until you have divided in each place. Write the remainder next to the quotient. Remember that the remainder must be less than the divisor.

**Examples:**

```
       53                    356 R2                   262 R4
   6)318                 7)2,494                  28)7,340
    -30                   -21                       -56
     18                    39                       174
    -18                   -35                      -168
      0                    44                        60
                         -42                        -56
                           2                          4
```

**It's Your Turn!**

**1.** 7)448

**2.** 17)38

**3.** 5)902

**4.** 4)3,805

**5.** 12)389

**6.** 25)918

**7.** 41)2,847

**8.** 79)4,902

**9.** 63)19,331

# Fractions

A fraction is a number that shows how many parts out of a whole. The top number is called the numerator. It tells how many parts. The whole, or total number of parts, is indicated by the number in the denominator. Examples of fractions include $\frac{1}{3}$, $\frac{7}{9}$, and $\frac{5}{2}$.

Equivalent fractions are fractions that have the same value. For example, some fractions that are equivalent to $\frac{1}{2}$ include $\frac{2}{4}$, $\frac{3}{6}$, $\frac{4}{8}$, and $\frac{5}{10}$. To find equivalent fractions, multiply the numerator and the denominator by the same number, or common factor.

**Examples:**

Find three fractions that are equivalent to $\frac{2}{3}$.

$$\frac{2 \times 2}{3 \times 2} = \frac{4}{6}; \ \frac{2 \times 5}{3 \times 5} = \frac{10}{15}; \ \frac{2 \times 8}{3 \times 8} = \frac{16}{24}$$

**It's Your Turn!**

1. Find three fractions that are equivalent to $\frac{2}{5}$.
2. Find three fractions that are equivalent to $\frac{4}{7}$.
3. What fraction has a denominator of 9 and is equivalent to $\frac{2}{3}$?
4. What fraction has a denominator of 24 and is equivalent to $\frac{1}{6}$?

Just as you can find equivalent fractions by multiplying by a common factor, you can reduce fractions by dividing the numerator and the denominator by a common factor.

When the greatest common factor of the numerator and denominator is 1, the fraction is in simplest form.

**Example:**

$\frac{18}{30} = \frac{18 \div 2}{30 \div 2} = \frac{9}{15}$, so $\frac{18}{30}$ can be reduced to $\frac{9}{15}$. But 9 and 15 have a common factor that is greater than 1. That common factor is 3. To reduce the fraction to its simplest form, $\frac{9 \div 3}{15 \div 3} = \frac{3}{5}$. The greatest common factor of 3 and 5 is 1, so the fraction is in simplest form.

**It's Your Turn!**

Write each fraction in simplest form.

5. $\frac{4}{10}$

6. $\frac{15}{45}$

7. $\frac{9}{63}$

8. $\frac{55}{99}$

9. $\frac{72}{144}$

10. $\frac{39}{143}$

11. $\frac{30}{75}$

12. $\frac{12}{144}$

13. $\frac{35}{45}$

# Add and Subtract Fractions

To add or subtract fractions, you need to:

- Check to see if the fractions have like (same) denominators. If not, rename the fractions using what you know about how to write equivalent fractions.
- Add or subtract the numerators. Keep the denominator the same.
- Simplify the sum or difference, if necessary. If the sum or difference is an improper fraction, rewrite it as a mixed number.

**Examples:**

$$\frac{1}{7} + \frac{3}{7} = \frac{4}{7} \qquad\qquad \frac{1}{12} + \frac{5}{12} = \frac{6}{12} = \frac{1}{2}$$

$$\frac{5}{6} + \frac{3}{6} = \frac{8}{6} = 1\frac{2}{6} = 1\frac{1}{3} \qquad\qquad \frac{7}{9} - \frac{5}{9} = \frac{2}{9}$$

$$\frac{5}{8} - \frac{3}{8} = \frac{2}{8} = \frac{1}{4} \qquad\qquad \frac{15}{4} - \frac{7}{4} = \frac{8}{4} = 2$$

$$\frac{1}{2} + \frac{2}{3} = \frac{3}{6} + \frac{4}{6} = \frac{7}{6} = 1\frac{1}{6} \qquad\qquad \frac{5}{4} - \frac{1}{3} = \frac{15}{12} - \frac{4}{12} = \frac{11}{12}$$

**It's Your Turn!**

Find each sum or difference.

1. $\dfrac{3}{5} + \dfrac{1}{5}$         2. $\dfrac{5}{8} + \dfrac{3}{8}$        3. $\dfrac{1}{9} + \dfrac{2}{9}$

4. $\dfrac{3}{10} + \dfrac{9}{10}$        5. $\dfrac{8}{7} - \dfrac{3}{7}$        6. $\dfrac{5}{6} - \dfrac{1}{6}$

7. $\dfrac{9}{15} - \dfrac{2}{15}$        8. $\dfrac{5}{14} - \dfrac{3}{14}$        9. $\dfrac{1}{2} + \dfrac{3}{8}$

10. $\dfrac{5}{6} + \dfrac{3}{4}$        11. $\dfrac{11}{15} + \dfrac{2}{3}$        12. $\dfrac{4}{7} + \dfrac{1}{6}$

13. $\dfrac{4}{7} - \dfrac{2}{5}$        14. $\dfrac{3}{5} - \dfrac{2}{6}$        15. $\dfrac{7}{8} - \dfrac{1}{3}$

16. $\dfrac{16}{18} - \dfrac{7}{9}$        17. $\dfrac{5}{8} + \dfrac{1}{3}$        18. $\dfrac{3}{7} - \dfrac{1}{4}$

# Decimals

To convert a decimal to a fraction, you need to:

- Write the decimal as a fraction. The decimal number goes in the numerator. The denominator is the place value of the decimal (tenths, hundredths, etc.).
- Simplify the fraction, if necessary.

**Examples:**

$$0.3 = \frac{3}{10} \qquad 0.47 = \frac{47}{100} \qquad 0.863 = \frac{863}{1,000}$$

$$0.5 = \frac{5}{10} = \frac{1}{2} \qquad 0.75 = \frac{75}{100} = \frac{3}{4} \qquad 0.125 = \frac{125}{1,000} = \frac{1}{8}$$

**It's Your Turn!**

Convert each decimal to a fraction. Simplify, if necessary.

| | | |
|---|---|---|
| **1.** 0.7 | **2.** 0.59 | **3.** 0.313 |
| **4.** 0.45 | **5.** 0.625 | **6.** 0.64 |
| **7.** 0.2 | **8.** 0.825 | **9.** 0.22 |

Not every fraction converts to a one-, two-, or three-digit decimal. The fraction $\frac{1}{3}$, for example, is equal to 0.33..., where the digit 3 repeats indefinitely.

It will help you to recognize the following fractions and their decimal conversions. The symbol "$\approx$" means "approximately equal to."

$$\frac{1}{4} = 0.25 \qquad \frac{1}{2} = 0.5 \qquad \frac{3}{4} = 0.75$$

$$\frac{1}{3} \approx 0.33... \qquad \frac{2}{3} \approx 0.66...$$

$$\frac{1}{5} = 0.2 \qquad \frac{2}{5} = 0.4 \qquad \frac{3}{5} = 0.6 \qquad \frac{4}{5} = 0.8$$

$$\frac{1}{8} = 0.125 \qquad \frac{3}{8} = 0.375 \qquad \frac{5}{8} = 0.625 \qquad \frac{7}{8} = 0.875$$

$$\frac{1}{10} = 0.1 \qquad \frac{3}{10} = 0.3 \qquad \frac{7}{10} = 0.7 \qquad \frac{9}{10} = 0.9$$

**It's Your Turn!**

Convert these fractions to decimals.

| | | | | |
|---|---|---|---|---|
| **10.** $\frac{1}{4}$ | **11.** $\frac{2}{3}$ | **12.** $\frac{4}{10}$ | **13.** $\frac{6}{10}$ | **14.** $\frac{1}{2}$ |

# Operations with Decimals

To add or subtract decimals, you need to:

- Align the decimals by their decimal points.
- If necessary, add placeholder zeroes so that each decimal has the same number of places.
- Follow the steps for adding and subtracting whole numbers.
- Place a decimal point in the sum or difference in the same place.

**Examples:**

```
     1 1                    10                           1 1
                       2 11 12  8 12
     4.3               3 1 2 . 9 2                       45.77
  + 16.9              - 1 6 8 . 4 7                     +  5.3
  ------              -----------                       ------
   2 1.2               1 4 4 . 4 5                       51.07
```

**It's Your Turn!**

**1.**  5.06
    + 7.44

**2.**  21.388
    + 22.749

**3.**  9.073
    − 6.78

**4.** 18.4
    − 5.82

**5.**  90.6
    + 115.925

**6.**  212.96
    − 185.71

To multiply decimals or to divide a decimal by a whole number, you need to:

- Follow the steps for multiplying or dividing whole numbers.
- When multiplying decimals, find the total number of digits to the right of the decimal point in each factor. This tells you the number of digits to the right of the decimal point in the product. Count over the number of places from the right and place the decimal point.
- When dividing a decimal by a whole number, put a decimal point in the quotient in the same place as the decimal point in the dividend.

**Examples:**

```
    1.4         5.3         2.73           12.2              46.37
  ×   8       × 6.2       × 8.1         7)85.4          13)602.81
  -----       -----       -----         -7               -52
   11.2         106         273         ----             ----
               3180       21840           15               82
               ----       -----         -14              -78
              32.86       22.113        ----             ----
                                          14               48
                                        -14              -39
                                        ----             ----
                                           0               91
                                                          -91
                                                          ----
                                                             0
```

**It's Your Turn!**

**7.** 5.6
    × 4

**8.**  2.1
    × 2.9

**9.**  7.17
    × 6.3

**10.** 4)144.8

**11.** 5)162.95

**12.** 36)824.76

# Ratios and Percents

A ratio is a comparison between a part and a whole. A ratio can be stated in words, with symbols, or as a fraction. The following expressions all indicate the same ratio:

$$1 \text{ to } 2 \qquad 1:2 \qquad \frac{1}{2}$$

A percent is a ratio that tells how many out of 100, and it is indicated by the symbol %. To find a percent when you know a fraction, find an equivalent fraction with a denominator of 100. For example, $\frac{1}{2} = \frac{50}{100}$, so $\frac{1}{2} = 50\%$.

To change a decimal to a percent, simply move the decimal point over two places to the left and add the %. For example, $0.5 = 50\%$.

Convert between ratios, decimals, fractions, and percents by applying their definitions. It may also help you to remember common conversions.

$25\% = 0.25 = \frac{1}{4}$      $33\% \approx 0.33... \approx \frac{1}{3}$      $50\% = 0.5 = \frac{1}{2}$

$66\% \approx 0.66 \approx \frac{2}{3}$      $75\% = 0.75 = \frac{3}{4}$      $100\% = 1$

**Examples:**

- Convert 45% to a fraction in simplest form. $45\% = \frac{45}{100} = \frac{9}{20}$
- Convert the ratio 10 : 15 to a fraction in simplest form. $10 \text{ to } 15 = \frac{10}{15} = \frac{2}{3}$
- Convert 83% to a decimal. $83\% = 0.83$

**It's Your Turn!**

1. Convert 37% to a fraction in simplest form.

2. Convert $\frac{2}{5}$ to a percent.

3. Convert 15% to a fraction in simplest form.

4. Convert the ratio 4 : 8 to a percent.

5. Convert 0.63 to a percent.

6. Convert 16% to a decimal.

7. Convert 0.24 to a fraction in simplest form.

8. Convert the ratio 3 : 9 to a percent.

# Basic Shapes

Understanding the properties of basic shapes and how to work with them is an important skill. Some common basic shapes and their properties are reviewed below.

### Circle

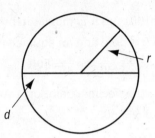

### Square

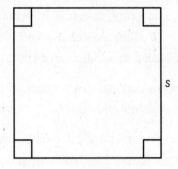

- The radius ($r$) is the distance from the center to any point on the circle.
- The diameter ($d$) is the width of the circle, and is equal to two times the radius.
- Circumference = $\pi d$
- Area = $\pi r^2$

- Has four equal sides ($s$)
- Has four angles, each of which measures 90°
- Perimeter = $4s$
- Area = $s^2$

### Rectangle

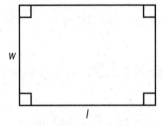

### Triangle

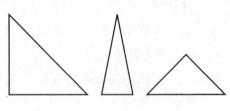

- Has two pairs of equal sides: length ($l$) and width ($w$)
- Has four 90° angles
- Perimeter = $2l + 2w$
- Area = $l \times w$

- Has three sides and three angles
- Perimeter = $a + b + c$
- Area = $\frac{1}{2}$(base × height)

**It's Your Turn!**

1. Which figure has four equal sides and four equal angles?

2. How do you find the perimeter of a triangle?

3. When finding the circumference of a circle, do you use the measure of the radius or the diameter?

4. How do you find the area of a rectangle?

# Answer Key

**Addition** *(p. 12)*

**1.** 73 **2.** 77 **3.** 1,620 **4.** 634 **5.** 788 **6.** 1,120

**Subtraction** *(p. 12)*

**1.** 19 **2.** 67 **3.** 28 **4.** 22 **5.** 587 **6.** 3,262

**Multiplication** *(p. 13)*

**1.** 72 **2.** 232 **3.** 1,188 **4.** 1,032 **5.** 5,280 **6.** 8,082 **7.** 672 **8.** 4,416 **9.** 8,664
**10.** 7,622 **11.** 109,174 **12.** 287,095

**Division** *(p. 14)*

**1.** 64 **2.** 2 R 4 **3.** 180 R 2 **4.** 951 R 1 **5.** 32 R 5 **6.** 36 R 18 **7.** 69 R 18 **8.** 62 R 4
**9.** 306 R 53

**Fractions** *(p. 15)*

**1.** Possible answers: $\frac{4}{10}$, $\frac{6}{15}$, $\frac{8}{20}$ **2.** Possible answers: $\frac{8}{14}$, $\frac{12}{21}$, $\frac{16}{28}$ **3.** $\frac{6}{9}$ **4.** $\frac{4}{24}$
**5.** $\frac{2}{5}$ **6.** $\frac{1}{3}$ **7.** $\frac{1}{7}$ **8.** $\frac{5}{9}$ **9.** $\frac{1}{2}$ **10.** $\frac{3}{11}$ **11.** $\frac{2}{5}$ **12.** $\frac{1}{12}$ **13.** $\frac{7}{9}$

**Add and Subtract Fractions** *(p. 16)*

**1.** $\frac{4}{5}$ **2.** 1 **3.** $\frac{1}{3}$ **4.** $1\frac{1}{5}$ **5.** $\frac{5}{7}$ **6.** $\frac{2}{3}$ **7.** $\frac{7}{15}$ **8.** $\frac{1}{7}$ **9.** $\frac{7}{8}$ **10.** $1\frac{7}{12}$ **11.** $1\frac{2}{5}$ **12.** $\frac{31}{42}$
**13.** $\frac{6}{35}$ **14.** $\frac{4}{15}$ **15.** $\frac{13}{24}$ **16.** $\frac{1}{9}$ **17.** $\frac{23}{24}$ **18.** $\frac{5}{28}$

**Decimals** *(p. 17)*

**1.** $\frac{7}{10}$ **2.** $\frac{59}{100}$ **3.** $\frac{313}{1,000}$ **4.** $\frac{9}{20}$ **5.** $\frac{5}{8}$ **6.** $\frac{16}{25}$ **7.** $\frac{1}{5}$ **8.** $\frac{33}{40}$ **9.** $\frac{11}{50}$ **10.** 0.25 **11.** 0.66...
**12.** 0.4 **13.** 0.6 **14.** 0.5

**Operations with Decimals** *(p. 18)*

**1.** 12.50 **2.** 44.137 **3.** 2.293 **4.** 12.58 **5.** 206.525 **6.** 27.25 **7.** 22.4 **8.** 6.09
**9.** 45.171 **10.** 36.2 **11.** 32.59 **12** 22.91

**Ratios and Percents** *(p. 19)*

**1.** $\frac{37}{100}$ **2.** 40% **3.** $\frac{3}{20}$ **4.** 50% **5.** 63% **6.** 0.16 **7.** $\frac{6}{25}$ **8.** 33%

**Basic Shapes** *(p. 20)*

**1.** square **2.** Add the measure of the three sides. **3.** diameter
**4.** Multiply the length times the width.

If you need additional practice with these math skills, complete Steck-Vaughn's *Building Strategies for GED Success: Mathematics* before using this book.

# 1 Problem Solving

What kinds of problem-solving situations might you encounter in the workplace? How can you be an effective problem solver? In this chapter, you will learn the answers to these questions by focusing on a five-step problem-solving method. You will learn about skills and strategies that will help you solve different types of problems you may encounter in the workplace and every day.

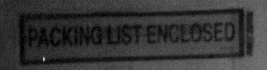

PACKING LIST ENCLOSED

# Get Started with Problem Solving

## Essential Tasks

**Determine what data is needed** to solve a problem or address a situation

**Determine whether to add, subtract, multiply, or divide** to solve a problem

## Build on What You Know

Think about a typical workday. What kinds of math problems do you need to solve? Maybe you need to calculate how many hours you worked in a week or how much you will need to budget for your electric bill during the summer.

Both in the workplace and in your daily life, you are continually solving different types of problems. From ensuring that your paycheck is correct to developing a work schedule to using the tools of measurement, good mathematical *problem-solving skills* are essential.

In this lesson, you will learn the first step of a problem-solving process you will use to solve mathematical problems, as well as other types of problems, in the workplace and in your daily life.

So how do you go about solving a problem either at work or in your daily life? You do it by taking one step at a time.

To solve any problem, you must:

1. **Understand the problem.** Understand what is being asked. Read carefully through the question. Find the key words and clues.

2. **Develop a plan.** Identify the information needed to solve the problem and the strategies that you will use.

3. **Work the plan.** Solve the problem using the strategies you selected.

4. **Check your results.** Reread the question. Check that your answer makes sense and adequately answers the question.

Throughout this text, you will be using these four steps as you solve different types of problems. Let's see how it works!

**Teacher Reminder**
Review the teacher lesson at
www.mysteckvaughn.com/WORK

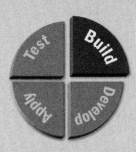

## In Real Life    What to Do?

Gladys is getting ready for work and is behind schedule. When she goes to the garage, she finds that her car will not start. Gladys has an important meeting this morning in which she is responsible for a presentation about how to reduce absenteeism among employees. Gladys looks at her watch and knows that she must be at work in an hour. Now she must decide how she will get to work on time.

 **With a classmate, discuss the following questions. Share your ideas with the class.**

1. What is Gladys's problem?

2. What options should Gladys explore to help her solve her problem successfully?

### Workplace Tip

Did you discuss that Gladys cannot get to work because her car will not start and that Gladys could ask a friend for a ride or use public transportation?

Diego has a yearly budget of $2,000 to spend on advertising. He has already spent $\frac{2}{5}$ of the budget on fliers. By the end of the month, Diego needs to spend the rest of his budget or the money will be added to a general fund. He is looking at different marketing materials to purchase that would effectively support his company's goals. Posters would make a wonderful addition to his new advertising campaign, but they are expensive at $25 each. Diego is not sure what he should do next.

 **With a classmate, discuss the following questions. Share your ideas with the class.**

3. What is Diego's problem?

4. What math skills does Diego need to use to find the answer?

### Workplace Tip

In the workplace, you are not always presented with a specific question to answer. Instead, like Diego, you may need to identify the different questions that need to be answered in order to solve the problem.

# Develop Your Skills

The first step in effective problem solving is to understand what the question is asking. When reading math problems, ask yourself:

- What is the question asking? Restate the question in your own words.
- What are the key words?
- What do the key words mean?

## What Is the Question Asking?

You are planning a seminar for your company with a budget of $50 per person. You are planning on 35 people attending the seminar. After some research, you have come up with the following numbers:

| Accounts | Budgets | Invoices | | Print | | Refresh |

| ITEM | COST |
| --- | --- |
| Food and beverage | $12.50 per person |
| Meeting room rental fee | $350.00 |
| Printing and copying | $195.00 |
| Speaker's fee | $300.00 |
| Miscellaneous costs | $225.00 |

**Workplace Tip**

Rewrite what the question is asking in your own words. This helps you to better understand the question.

 **Using the figures above, what is the cost per person for the seminar?**

1. What is the question asking?

## What Are the Key Words?

When solving word problems, you will need to convert the problem into an equation. First, find the key words in the problem and then decide whether you will need to add, subtract, multiply, or divide.

**Example:**

After taxes, Gregorio makes $425 a week, and Claudine makes $375. What is their **combined** income? *The key word **combined** refers to addition. In this problem, you would add: $425 + $375 = $800.*

**Example:**

Abby operates a private daycare center where she employs eight workers. Abby has $14,780 in her checking account and a payroll of $9,389. How much money does she have **left** after she pays her staff? **The key word *left*** *means to subtract. In this problem, you subtract: $14,780 − $9,389 = $5,391.*

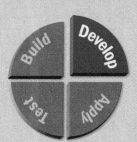

**Example:**

Philipe manages an apartment complex where he collects $755 per month for each apartment. In January, Philipe will raise the rent on each apartment **by** 8%. How much more will Philipe receive in rent for each apartment? *The key word **by** means to multiply. In this problem, you multiply: $755 × 8% = $60.40 more a month for each apartment.*

**Example:**

You work in the shipping department for a large distribution center. Each day the center receives 5,715 boxes of produce to be **split** into 45 equal shipments. How many boxes will be in each shipment? *The key word **split** refers to division. In this problem, you divide: $\frac{5,715}{45} = 127$.*

These are not the only words that indicate each operation. With experience, you will learn to identify many different types of key words.

---

| In Real Life | **A Lot of Talk** |

You are working on a productivity report for your telemarketing company. In the past year, you note that the 109 telemarketers employed by the company spent 8,943 hours talking to prospective customers. The report asks for the average number of hours spent by each telemarketer talking to prospective customers.

 **Imagine you are asked to complete the report. How would you calculate the required information? Ask yourself the following questions.**

   **2.** What is the question asking?

   **3.** What are the key words?

   **4.** What number operation would you use to solve?

---

**GOT IT?** | **To improve your mathematical problem-solving skills, you should first understand what the problem is asking by:**

- Rewriting the question in your own words.
- Identifying the key words in the problem.
- Identifying the different operations that you will use to solve the problem.

# Apply Your Knowledge

Solving workplace math problems requires that you use your problem-solving skills.

**As you read the following scenarios, think about the problem-solving strategies that you learned in this lesson. Answer the three key questions and then solve the problem.**

1.  Yelena is framing a picture for a customer. She has a piece of picture frame molding that is 58 inches long. The job requires 47 inches of molding. How much molding will Yelena have left after framing the picture?

    • What is the question asking?

    • What are the key words?

    • What number operations would you use to solve?

    A. 11 in.

    B 47 in.

    C. 58 in.

    D. 105 in.

2.  Iman delivers mail for the local postal service. Iman would like to know the average number of pieces of mail she delivers each day. She works 6 days a week and in the past week delivered 26,346 pieces of mail. How many pieces of mail does Iman deliver on an average day?

    • What is the question asking?

    • What are the key words?

    • What number operations would you use to solve?

    A. 4,391

    B. 26,340

    C. 26,352

    D. 158,076

## In Real Life   Put Your Skills to Work!

You have been offered a chance to work as an assistant to the marketing team on a new advertising campaign. You have been hoping for a chance to put your art skills to work. The new job will require longer hours, but your salary will go from $12 per hour to $15 per hour, and you'll have a chance to earn overtime pay when you work more than 40 hours a week. Your children are in school, but you will need to pay for after-school child care, especially when you work overtime. There is a job opening in another department that won't require overtime, but your salary would increase to only $13 per hour.

 **Think about the problem you are facing and put your skills to work! Which job will you choose? Provide reasons for your answer.**

### Workplace Tip

When making your decision, did you think about the:

- Hourly wages?
- Child care costs?
- Total hours worked?
- Future career potential?
- Job satisfaction?

## Think About It!

**When you encounter a math problem at work, what is your first step in solving the problem?**

**What problems in the workplace have required you to use your math skills?**

**What specific math skills did you use?**

Remember, math is all about problem solving. The first step in solving any problem is to have a good understanding of all aspects of the problem, including what questions need to be answered. Everyone uses math in the workplace, whether they realize it or not. However, unlike the questions that you see in a textbook, real-world math problems don't always provide you with the specific question to be answered or a list of answers from which to choose. It is important to be an effective problem solver so that you can apply your mathematical skills to workplace situations.

**Answer Key**

1. A
2. A

# Test Your WRC Skills

**Read the following situations. Select which answer you think is the correct response.**

**1.** You have been hired as a sales representative for a national book company. Your job requires a great deal of travel each month. You get reimbursed $0.50 for each mile that you drive. This past month you drove 2,348 miles. How much will you invoice your company for mileage?

| | | |
|---|---|---|
| **A.** | ○ | $11.74 |
| **B.** | ○ | $117.40 |
| **C.** | ○ | $1,174.00 |
| **D.** | ○ | $2,348.00 |

**2.** You are making a pair of curtains for a customer. The material that the customer has selected for the curtains will cost you $138. For each order, you also charge an additional $50 for your labor and $28 for supplies. How much will you charge your customer?

| | | |
|---|---|---|
| **A.** | ○ | $78 |
| **B.** | ○ | $138 |
| **C.** | ○ | $188 |
| **D.** | ○ | $216 |

**3.** You work in the stockroom of a grocery store chain where you must document shipments received. You have just received a shipment of 80 boxes of canned vegetables. Each box contains 144 cans. How many cans of vegetables did you receive?

| | | |
|---|---|---|
| **A.** | ○ | 144 |
| **B.** | ○ | 224 |
| **C.** | ○ | 1,152 |
| **D.** | ○ | 11,520 |

**4.** A customer comes into the restaurant where you work. Your customer purchases two hamburgers that cost $2.99 each, one order of fries for $1.69, and two large drinks that cost $1.89 each. How much does the customer owe before tax is added?

| | | |
|---|---|---|
| **A.** | ○ | $6.57 |
| **B.** | ○ | $9.56 |
| **C.** | ○ | $11.45 |
| **D.** | ○ | $13.14 |

5. You are making copies of handouts for a department-wide meeting. There are 27 people in your department, and there are three different handouts that each person will need. If you don't make any extras, how many total copies will you make?

| | | |
|---|---|---|
| **A.** | ○ | 9 |
| **B.** | ○ | 30 |
| **C.** | ○ | 81 |
| **D.** | ○ | 243 |

6. You work as a groomer in a pet store. You groomed 46 animals in May, 39 animals in June, 39 animals in July, and 26 animals in August. How many animals have you groomed in the last four months?

| | | |
|---|---|---|
| **A.** | ○ | 43 |
| **B.** | ○ | 111 |
| **C.** | ○ | 150 |
| **D.** | ○ | 2,157 |

7. You have been working at the same job for the last twelve months. During that time, you have been depositing $50 each month from your paycheck into a special account so that you can buy a new television that costs $575. How much money have you saved in the last twelve months?

| | | |
|---|---|---|
| **A.** | ○ | $525 |
| **B.** | ○ | $575 |
| **C.** | ○ | $600 |
| **D.** | ○ | $625 |

8. Carlos works as an administrative assistant. One of his tasks is to order supplies for his company. He wants to purchase 36 boxes of pens that are on sale for $12.99 per box. How much will the pens cost?

| | | |
|---|---|---|
| **A.** | ○ | $12.99 |
| **B.** | ○ | $48.99 |
| **C.** | ○ | $432.00 |
| **D.** | ○ | $467.64 |

Check your answers on page 145.

# Identify What Information Is Needed

## Essential Tasks

**Determine what data is needed** to solve a problem or address a situation.

**Determine whether to add, subtract, multiply, or divide** to solve a problem.

## Build on What You Know

Many times in the workplace and in daily life, you deal with multiple facts or large amounts of information. Some facts and information are **relevant** to what you are doing and some are **irrelevant**. Relevant information is related or connected to the problem that you are trying to solve or the task you are trying to complete. Irrelevant information is the opposite: it has no connection to the task or is not necessary to solve the problem.

What are some examples in everyday life where you are given information that is irrelevant to the task you are trying to complete? Maybe you are trying to make plans with a friend. You need to know where and when to meet, but your friend is telling you where she needs to stop beforehand.

In work and in life, you must continually sort through information to determine what is relevant and what is not. You must determine what information you need in order to complete the task or project. You may also be asked to complete a task for which you need more information. In this lesson, you will learn how to read a problem that includes information that is irrelevant to the solution. You will sort though the facts to determine which are needed. You will also identify whether a problem is missing information and what facts are needed to solve it.

### In Real Life  What Do I Need to Know?

You are asked to order office supplies. The following spreadsheet is posted in the office copy room.

| Item | Number | Cost | Person Asking |
|---|---|---|---|
| Hanging file folders | 2 boxes | $128.00/box | Jamilla |
| 3-ring binders, $8\frac{1}{2} \times 11$ | 5 | $17.89 each | Han |
| Self-stick notes | 20 packs | $22.65/pack | Roberta |
| $8\frac{1}{2} \times 11$ copy paper | 7 boxes | $169.00/box | Ranjit |

**Teacher Reminder**
Review the teacher lesson at
www.mysteckvaughn.com/WORK

**32** Math

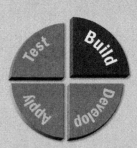

 **With a classmate, discuss the following questions. Share your ideas with the class.**

1. What are you trying to determine?

2. What information do you need to be able to place the order?

3. Is there information that is irrelevant to the problem?

The first problem-solving step is to understand what the question is asking. The second step is to develop a plan to solve the problem. To do this, you need to identify the information needed to solve the problem.

 **Look at the following chart. Put a check mark in the appropriate box. Discuss your results with the class.**

| Information | Relevant | Irrelevant |
| --- | --- | --- |
| Items to be ordered | | |
| Number of each item needed | | |
| Cost of each item | | |
| Name of Person Requesting Item | | |

After you have figured out how to categorize information to solve a problem, you may realize there is information you need that you don't have.

## In Real Life   What Is Missing?

You are stacking boxes of groceries at a storage warehouse. Each box weighs 25 pounds. You have been stacking for about 15 minutes. Each shelf can hold a maximum of 500 pounds. How many more boxes can you stack on the shelf?

 **With a classmate, discuss the following questions. Share your ideas with the class.**

4. What are you trying to determine?

5. What information do you need to determine how many more boxes you can stack on the shelf?

6. Is there information that is irrelevant to the problem?

> **Workplace Tip**
> Did you discuss the importance of the fact that some boxes are already stacked on the shelf? Did you decide that the time spent stacking (15 minutes) is irrelevant to the question?

# Develop Your Skills

Before you begin solving a problem, read the entire problem carefully. It may help you to follow these steps when problem solving:

- Determine the question you are trying to answer.
- Identify the facts that are important to answering the question by underlining or circling them.
- Cross out any facts that are irrelevant to the question.
- Determine if there is necessary information that is not given in the problem.

## Relevant and Irrelevant Information

You work in the lumber department at a home-improvement store. You need to create a sales brochure for your department. The brochure needs to include the size of each board. Jackie told you that there are 30 boards per stack.

**Using the scenario above, what information is missing that is necessary for the sales guide?**

1. What do you need to know?

2. What fact is irrelevant to the problem?

## What Information Is Missing?

When solving problems, you need to identify what information is needed to solve the problem and also what facts and information are irrelevant or unrelated to the problem. You also need to be able to recognize if any needed information is missing from the problem.

**Example:**

You are planning a job that involves laying square bricks to form a patio. You know that you will need 75 bricks to complete the patio. One package of the bricks costs $25. What information do you need to know in order to buy the correct number of packages? *You must know the number of bricks sold in a package.*

**Example:**

The manager of the store has asked you buy enough juice to restock the juice machine. What must you know before you order the juice? *You must determine how much of each juice is needed to fill the machine.*

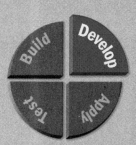

**Example:**

Max has worked at the store one year longer than you. The difference between what you earn and what Max earns is $1.10 per hour. What information do you need to know in order to figure out how much you will probably earn in one year? *You must know how much you earn per hour now, so you can add $1.10 to it.*

**Example:**

Carson works 40 hours per week for a landscape company. He is rewarded for good work by receiving a 5% raise. What do you need to know in order to figure what Carson earns after the raise? *You must know Carson's earnings before the raise.*

## In Real Life    Savings Add Up

You have been working for Countryside Painters for 3 years. Your schedule changed last year, so now you work Tuesday through Saturday each week. Each month, you have deposited part of your paycheck into a savings account. In addition, you deposited your annual bonus of $500. You received the bonus only one year.

 **You just received your most recent bank statement. Assume you have never withdrawn any money from the account. How can you confirm that the account balance shown on your statement is correct?**

3. What information is not relevant to the question?

4. What needed information is missing from the problem in order to answer it?

5. How would you answer the question if you were given the necessary information?

### GOT IT?    In order to solve a mathematical problem, you must examine the facts given to determine:

- If you have all of the facts necessary to answer the question.

- If some of the information is irrelevant to the problem.

- What other information is required to answer the question.

 **To Do List**
Remember to follow these steps when applying your knowledge:

❑ **Read the problem carefully to identify the question.**

❑ **Underline or circle the important facts.**

❑ **Identify any facts that are irrelevant and cross them out.**

❑ **Identify any missing information.**

# Apply Your Knowledge

Solving real-world problems often involves identifying the relevant, irrelevant, and missing information.

**As you read the following scenarios, think about the relevance of the given information. Answer the key questions and determine what information is missing.**

1. The passenger bus you are driving gets about 7 miles per gallon of fuel. You are scheduled to drive 1,500 miles this week. You drive 350 miles on the first day. What information must you have to determine the number of times you will have to get fuel this week?

   • What is the problem asking?

   • What facts are relevant to the question?

   • What facts, if any, are irrelevant to the question?

   **A.** the number of days you will drive in the week

   **B** the number of passengers you will transport

   **C.** how many gallons of fuel the tank holds

   **D.** how much luggage the passengers will bring

2. The shipping company charges extra for each box that weighs more than 15 pounds. You are packing sample toothbrushes to send to dentists throughout the state. What information about the contents of each box is most important?

   • What is the problem asking?

   • What facts are relevant to the question?

   • What facts, if any, are irrelevant to the question?

   **A.** the number of toothbrushes in each box

   **B.** the weight of the toothbrushes in each box

   **C.** the color of the toothbrushes shipped out

   **D.** the number of boxes shipped out

**Put Your Skills to Work!**

You are a trainer at a rehabilitation clinic. You are reviewing the exercise program a doctor has ordered for a recovering patient. The doctor has ordered 30 minutes of exercise 5 days per week. The patient is to exercise at his target heart rate as shown in the table below provided by the doctor.

| Age (Years) | Target Heart Rate Range (Beats Per Minute) |
|---|---|
| 20 | 140–170 |
| 30 | 133–162 |
| 40 | 126–153 |
| 50 | 119–145 |
| 60 | 112–136 |
| 70 | 105–128 |

 **Think about the problem you are facing and put your skills to work! How can you determine the correct heart rate range? Explain your answer.**

**Workplace Tip**

When you determined which information was missing, did you:

- Examine the table carefully?
- Circle or underline the information you will need to solve?
- Cross out any irrelevant information?
- Identify the missing information?

## Think About It!

**What situations at work required you to sort through information to determine what was relevant and what was irrelevant?**

**Have you had instances at work where you were solving a problem in which some necessary facts were missing? How did you overcome this obstacle?**

Remember that every math problem requires certain relevant information in order to solve the problem. It is important to read each problem carefully, identify irrelevant information, and determine what information is missing. Once you know what other information is needed, you can take steps to find the information. This is an important skill if you are going to be a problem solver in the workplace.

# Test Your WRC Skills

**Solving mathematical problems requires that you use different problem-solving strategies. Read the following situations. Select which answer you think is the correct response.**

**1.** A tractor trailer can legally carry up to 8,000 pounds. You are using a forklift to load shipping containers onto the trailer. What information is most important about the containers?

| | | |
|---|---|---|
| **A.** | ○ | the volume of each container |
| **B.** | ○ | the number of containers that will fit on the trailer |
| **C.** | ○ | the weight of each container |
| **D.** | ○ | the color of each container |

**2.** You are stocking 1-gallon containers of milk on 6 shelves in the refrigerator in the dairy section of the grocery store. You can place 16 gallons on each shelf. One-half of the shelves are already stocked. You are wheeling in crates of milk to restock the shelves. What additional information do you need before you start wheeling crates into the store?

| | | |
|---|---|---|
| **A.** | ○ | the volume of each milk container |
| **B.** | ○ | the weight of each crate of milk |
| **C.** | ○ | the number of gallons on each shelf |
| **D.** | ○ | the number of gallons in each crate |

**3.** You are delivering mulch to a nursery. They have requested 1,500 bags of mulch. You must load complete pallets of mulch onto the delivery truck. Before you start loading the truck, what additional information is needed?

| | | |
|---|---|---|
| **A.** | ○ | the number of bags of mulch on each pallet |
| **B.** | ○ | the weight of mulch on each pallet |
| **C.** | ○ | the distance to the nursery |
| **D.** | ○ | the volume of each pallet of mulch |

**4.** You supervisor has asked you to order office supplies for your entire department. You examine the previous orders and check the current supply drawer. You find that the office has used 32 reams of paper, there are 33 of the 100 pens ordered left, and the delivery department has used 127 gallons of fuel for their delivery vans. Your supervisor would like to order 2 additional boxes of letterhead this month. What information is irrelevant to the task you have been assigned?

| | | |
|---|---|---|
| **A.** | ○ | The office has used 32 reams of paper. |
| **B.** | ○ | There are 33 of the 100 pens ordered left. |
| **C.** | ○ | The delivery department has used 127 gallons of fuel for their delivery vans. |
| **D.** | ○ | Your supervisor would like to order 2 additional boxes of letterhead this month. |

**5.** The library you work at is shifting the books around to add a new reading area. You are using a cart to remove encyclopedias from one bookshelf and take them to a different location in the library. Each bookshelf where the encyclopedias will be placed can hold 18 encyclopedias. There are 216 encyclopedias total. What information is needed to determine how many trips you will need to take?

| | | |
|---|---|---|
| **A.** | ○ | the weight of each encyclopedia |
| **B.** | ○ | how many encyclopedias will fit on the cart |
| **C.** | ○ | the order of the encyclopedias |
| **D.** | ○ | the distance between the bookshelves |

**6.** You are collecting money from vending machines on your route. You collected $176.50 and $122.75 from the first two stops. At the third stop, you collected $158.00 and the customer ordered $125.00 more in product. Which of the following dollar amounts should not be used in finding the total collected for the day?

| | | |
|---|---|---|
| **A.** | ○ | $122.75 |
| **B.** | ○ | $125.00 |
| **C.** | ○ | $158.00 |
| **D.** | ○ | $176.50 |

**7.** You are in a factory that assembles office chairs. Each line can assemble 100 chairs per shift. What additional information do you need to determine the number of chairs assembled per shift at the factory?

| | | |
|---|---|---|
| **A.** | ○ | the number of lines at the factory |
| **B.** | ○ | the speed of each worker on the line |
| **C.** | ○ | the number of chairs ordered |
| **D.** | ○ | the number of workers on the line |

**8.** You are painting four sides of a building that are all the same size. Before you buy the paint for the job, what additional information is needed in order to determine how much paint to buy?

| | | |
|---|---|---|
| **A.** | ○ | the amount of time it will take to finish |
| **B.** | ○ | the total square feet of wall that needs to be painted |
| **C.** | ○ | the number of painters that will be helping you |
| **D.** | ○ | the volume of the building |

Check your answers on page 146.

# Use Strategies to Problem Solve

## Essential Tasks

**Determine whether to add, subtract, multiply, or divide** to solve a problem

**Determine what data is needed** to solve a problem or address a situation

**Create simple expressions or formulas from real-life situations** or from tables

## Build on What You Know

Think about the last time you had a problem to solve. Could you think of more than one way to solve that problem? For example, you may have been in a meeting at work where different people presented different solutions to the same problem. Each of those solutions may have actually worked to solve the problem at hand, but usually one solution or strategy is chosen. A **strategy** is a plan that you develop in order to achieve a goal. In this case, your goal is to solve a given problem.

Identifying and being able to use different strategies to solve problems is an important skill. It is also helpful to be able to determine which strategy may help you solve the problem most efficiently or easily.

Once you have determined which strategy to use, remember to incorporate the problem-solving skills you have already learned:

- Read the problem carefully to identify the question being asked.
- Identify any key words that indicate what operation to use.
- Sort through the facts and information to determine what is relevant.

### In Real Life   What Is the Right Strategy?

A local business has hired the company you work for to wash all of the windows on their building for a special event. The event begins at 5:00 P.M. You need to plan the crew's work schedule so that they finish the job and are gone from the worksite by 4:30 P.M. You know that the crew will need 30 minutes to unpack the equipment and get set up to do the work. They will need 45 minutes to get cleaned up and packed up when the job is finished. From doing the job before, you know it will take the crew at most 3.5 hours to wash all of the windows. How can you determine what time the crew must begin in order to finish the work on time?

**Teacher Reminder**

Review the teacher lesson at www.mysteckvaughn.com/WORK

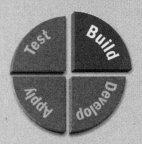

 **With a classmate, discuss the following questions. Share your ideas with the class.**

1. What is the problem you are trying to solve?

2. What are the important facts in this problem?

3. How can you organize the information you are given in order to develop a strategy to solve the problem?

4. What are some different strategies you could use to determine the correct starting time for the job?

**Workplace Tip**
Remember that restating the question in your own words, underlining relevant information, and crossing out irrelevant facts can help you organize information.

When solving problems in the workplace or in daily life, it is important to determine an appropriate strategy. Some problem-solving strategies include:

- Drawing a picture or diagram,
- Working backwards, and
- Using a formula (such as multiplying length times width to find the area of a rectangular space).

How do you determine which problem-solving strategy to use? Think about the problem-solving steps you have learned so far. After you have read and understood what the problem is asking, you sort the information given depending on whether it is relevant or irrelevant to the problem you are trying to solve.

Once you have completed these steps, the next step is to finish developing your plan for solving. This is where you will decide which strategy to use. Look at the information you will need to solve. How do you need to use that information? What do you need to do with that information? Your understanding of the question being asked is very important in helping you pick a problem-solving strategy. If you have identified any key words, use those to help you determine which strategy to use.

 **With a classmate, discuss the following questions. Share your ideas with the class.**

5. Write down each of the problem-solving strategies listed above. Can you think of a problem or situation, either at work or in daily life, where you would use each strategy?

6. Are there any other problem-solving strategies you have used?

# Develop Your Skills

There are many different strategies you can use to solve problems. The strategy you choose should be determined by the question being asked, the key words that give you clues about how to solve, and the relevant information in the problem. Some common problem-solving strategies are discussed below.

## Draw a Picture or Diagram

When you use the "draw a picture or diagram" strategy, you make a visual representation of the problem or organize the information in a way that makes it easier to understand. Read the scenario below and think about how you could use this strategy to solve the problem.

You work for a lawn maintenance and landscaping company as a planning clerk. There are 12 individuals on a work crew. The workers who mow earn $12 per hour. The workers who landscape earn $15 per hour. There are 8 members who mow, 4 who landscape and 2 that can do both. You have a landscape job that will require all of the members who can landscape to work for 6 hours.

 **Using the scenario above, how could you determine what the company's labor cost will be for the job?**

1. What do you need to know to determine the cost?

2. Is there any information in the problem that is irrelevant?

3. How can you use the "draw a picture or diagram" strategy to solve the problem?

## Work Backwards

The "work backwards" strategy is helpful when you know the end result but need to determine what you started with. Read the scenario below and think about how you could use this strategy to solve the problem.

At the end of his shift, Samuel had a total of $897.13 in his cash drawer. He had $512.22 in credit card sales and $234.91 in cash sales.

 **Using the scenario above, how could you figure out how much cash was in his drawer at the beginning of his shift?**

4. What operations will you use to solve the problem?

5. How can you use the "work backwards" strategy to solve the problem?

# Use a Formula

The "use a formula" strategy is helpful when solving problems involving measurement or geometry. To use this strategy, first determine the appropriate formula for what you need to find. Then substitute the numerical values in the correct place and perform the operation. Read the scenario below and think about how you could use this strategy to solve.

You are taking measurements to give a homeowner the cost of having carpet installed in the living room. The room is 13 feet long and 10 feet wide. You charge $3 per square foot for the carpet and installation.

 **Using the scenario above, what should you charge the customer?**

**6.** What do you need to know to determine the cost?

**7.** What formula do you need to use in order to determine the cost?

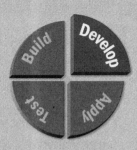

**Workplace Tip**
You could also draw a picture to help you visualize the problem.

## Choose a Strategy

Remember to identify key words and what you need to know to solve.

You are working at a sidewalk food cart downtown. The cost of each of the items you sell is shown on the price list to the right. A customer wants to purchase 2 hot dogs, a hot pretzel, a bottle of juice, and 3 bags of chips. How can you figure out what to charge the customer? If the customer gives you $20.00, how much change would you give him?

| Item | Price |
| --- | --- |
| Hot Dog | $1.50 |
| Hamburger | $2.00 |
| French Fries | $1.25 |
| Hot Pretzel | $0.75 |
| Bag of Chips | $1.00 |
| Bottle of Juice | $1.75 |
| Bottle of Water | $1.25 |

 **With a classmate, discuss the steps you would take to answer the questions.**

**GOT IT?**

**To successfully determine how to use a problem-solving strategy and which problem-solving strategy to use:**

- Be sure you understand what the question is asking.
- Identify the key words and important information in the problem.
- Choose a strategy that will help you solve the problem.

**Answer Key**
**1.** the number of workers who will be working on the job, the number of hours they will be working, and the rate they earn per hour
**2.** You do not need the information about the number of workers who mow or their hourly pay rate.
**3.** You could draw a diagram to help you determine the number of workers who mow, landscape, or do both.
**4.** addition and subtraction
**5.** You know the total amount that was in the cash drawer at the end of Samuel's shift. You can subtract the total credit card and cash sales from that amount to find the amount that was in his drawer at the start of his shift.
**6.** the area (square feet) of the room
**7.** area = length times width

**To Do List**

Remember to follow these steps when choosing a problem-solving strategy:

- ❑ **Read the problem carefully to identify the key words.**
- ❑ **Identify the operations that are necessary to solve the problem.**
- ❑ **Identify which strategy you want to use to solve the problem.**

# Apply Your Knowledge

Solving problems requires you to use different strategies. In order to solve real-world problems, you must determine what the question is asking and identify all operations necessary to solve the problem.

**As you read the following scenarios, think about which strategy you can use to solve the problem.**

1. You are driving a truck with boxes of cookies for delivery. If the average speed along your route is 40 miles per hour and you spend 5.5 hours of your work day driving, how far have you traveled at the end of your work day?

   A.  7.28 mi

   B.  34.5 mi

   C.  45.5 mi

   D.  220 mi

2. A carpenter placed an order for several lengths of 2 × 4s. He ordered four 6-foot, five 8-foot, and three 10-foot length boards. Using the price list shown below, what is the total cost of the lumber?

| Length (ft) | Price |
|---|---|
| 6 | $4.50 |
| 8 | $6.00 |
| 10 | $7.25 |
| 12 | $9.50 |

   A. $596.25

   B. $147.50

   C.  $69.75

   D.  $29.75

3. You are in charge of scheduling patients for the doctor that you work for. Her office is open for 8 hours on Thursday. The doctor's goal is to see 55 patients each Thursday. You have 5 patients scheduled per hour so far for this Thursday. How many patients do you still need to schedule to meet the goal for the day?

   A. 15

   B. 60

   C. 63

   D. 95

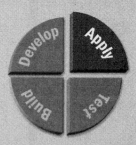

## In Real Life · Put Your Skills to Work!

You are working as a retail clerk at Pilsnera's Five-and-Dime Store. A customer buys 7 pieces of candy that are priced at $0.75 each and 4 pieces that are $0.20 each. All the customer has to pay with is a $10 bill.

 **Think about the problem you are facing and put your skills to work! How can you find the total cost of the candy? How can you find the amount of change you will give back to the customer?**

### Workplace Tip

When making your decision, did you:

- Read the problem and identify any key words?
- Identify all of the operations involved?
- Choose a strategy to help you solve?

## Think About It!

**What situations have you encountered at work that required you to determine a strategy to solve a problem?**

**Have you ever faced a problem that you could solve using more than one strategy? How did you decide which strategy to try first?**

**Have you ever selected a strategy that did not work as you thought it might? What did you do?**

When solving mathematical problems, you must read the problem carefully to determine what operations to use in finding the solution. Sometimes a picture, drawing, or diagram can help you better understand a problem. Oftentimes, multiple strategies will help you solve a problem in the workplace. When this is the case, it is still important to read and understand all of the facts that pertain to the problem. Some of the facts may be irrelevant and can be ignored. You must use all of your problem-solving skills in mathematics and the workplace.

**Answer Key**

1. D
2. C
3. A

# Test Your WRC Skills

Solving mathematical problems with multiple steps requires that you use a variety of strategies. Read the following situations. Select which answer you think is the correct response.

1. You are ordering supplies for the automotive shop where you work. You have ordered 20 boxes of motor oil. Each box contains eight 5-gallon bottles of oil. How many bottles of motor oil did you order?

| | | |
|---|---|---|
| A. | ○ | 2.5 |
| B. | ○ | 12 |
| C. | ○ | 28 |
| D. | ○ | 160 |

2. You are working the sales counter at a hardware store. A customer brings some merchandise to the counter to pay. He has 15 screws that cost $0.22 each, a hammer that costs $14.99, and 4 hooks that cost $1.29 each. What is the total cost of the purchase?

| | | |
|---|---|---|
| A. | ○ | $16.50 |
| B. | ○ | $35.50 |
| C. | ○ | $255.25 |
| D. | ○ | $23.45 |

3. You work at a newsstand that sells the items shown in the price list below. A customer would like to purchase a newspaper, 2 different maps, and 4 different magazines. What is the total cost of the purchase?

| Item | Price ($) |
|---|---|
| Newspaper | $1.75 |
| Magazine | $4.95 |
| Paperback | $9.95 |
| Map | $6.95 |

| | | |
|---|---|---|
| A. | ○ | $35.45 |
| B. | ○ | $38.45 |
| C. | ○ | $481.63 |
| D. | ○ | $13.65 |

4. You are responsible for buying bottled water for an outdoor community picnic. There are 450 people expected to attend. If each case of water contains 18 bottles, how many cases do you need to buy?

| A. | ○ | 8,100 |
|----|---|-------|
| B. | ○ | 25 |
| C. | ○ | 468 |
| D. | ○ | 432 |

5. You work on an assembly line in an auto plant earning $18 per hour. If you work over 40 hours per week, you earn $1\frac{1}{2}$ times your normal hourly wage for each hour. What are your earnings for a week in which you worked 45 hours?

| A. | ○ | $720.00 |
|----|---|---------|
| B. | ○ | $726.50 |
| C. | ○ | $811.50 |
| D. | ○ | $855.00 |

6. Your sales goal is to sell 35 pairs of shoes per week. You earn $20 for each pair you sell. If you meet your sales goal, you earn a bonus of $100. How much do you earn in a week in which you sell exactly 35 pairs of shoes?

| A. | ○ | $700 |
|----|---|------|
| B. | ○ | $800 |
| C. | ○ | $155 |
| D. | ○ | $600 |

7. You must travel to a plant to inspect some new equipment. The plant is 225 miles away from your office. If you travel an average speed of 60 miles per hour, how long will it take you to get to the plant?

| A. | ○ | 37.5 hr |
|----|---|---------|
| B. | ○ | 165 hr |
| C. | ○ | 3.75 hr |
| D. | ○ | 285 hr |

**Check your answers on page 147.**

# Solve the Problem

## Essential Tasks

**Determine whether to add, subtract, multiply or divide** to solve a problem

**Determine what data is needed** to solve a problem or address a situation

**Create simple expressions** or formulas from real-life situations or from tables

**Apply order of operations** in simple multi-step problems

## Build on What You Know

Do you have a friend or family member who speaks a foreign language? When they say something in one language and then repeat it in another language, they are **translating** from one language to another.

You often do this same kind of translation when you solve math problems. You take the numbers and other information, such as key words, and translate the problem into a mathematical **expression**. In math, an expression contains numbers, operation symbols, and sometimes variables to represent unknowns.

Think about a situation where you might have had to take written or verbal instruction and change it into a math expression. For example, suppose you work as a server at a restaurant. At the end of the night, you and the other servers are expected to give one-fifth of your tips to be divided equally among the hostess, bartender, and 2 bussers. How can you determine how much to give each person? You can translate the problem into a mathematical expression to help you.

### In Real Life  What Is the Cost?

You are working as a home health aid. Your supervisor calls and asks you to order 8 glucose monitors and 12 ice packs. She would like you to place the order and then e-mail her with the total cost.

You call the medical supply company and find that each glucose monitor costs $33.99, and each ice pack costs $14.85. To complete the task, you write down the number of each item you need to order and multiply that number by the price of each item. Then you add the cost of the items to find the total cost.

 **With a classmate, discuss the following questions. Share your ideas with the class.**

1. What are the important facts listed in the problem?

2. What operations were used to solve this problem?

3. Was the order in which the problem was solved important? Why or why not?

**Teacher Reminder**
Review the teacher lesson at
www.mysteckvaughn.com/WORK

# Translating Words into Mathematical Expressions

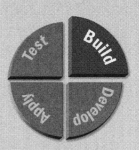

Translating a math problem into numbers and operation symbols is one of the final steps in the problem-solving process. Remember the steps you learned in Lesson 1:

1. **Understand the problem** Understand what is being asked. Read carefully through the question. Find the key words and clues.

2. **Develop a plan** Identify the information needed to solve the problem and the strategies that you will use.

3. **Work the plan** Solve the problem.

4. **Check your results** Reread the question. Check that your answer makes sense and adequately answers the question.

Finding key words and terms is very important when translating problems into mathematical expressions. In the example at the beginning of the lesson, the key terms were **one-fifth** and **divided equally**. "One-fifth" told you the fractional amount of your tips that you needed to give to others. "Divided equally" told you how to split that amount among each person who was to receive some money.

Below is a list of key words and the mathematical operation they may indicate. Being able to identify these key words can help you translate problems into math expressions.

| Key Word | Mathematical Operation |
|---|---|
| add, total, in all, all together, sum, combined, increased by | addition |
| difference, minus, take away, left over, how much left, how much change, how much more, how much less | subtraction |
| times, two/three times, multiplied by, each, apiece | multiplication |
| how much per, each, divided, shared equally, apiece, equal, how many equal groups | division |

These keywords may not always be present every time you need to solve a problem, but there may other clues within the problem that will help you.

 **Choose one word from the table to represent each operation. For each chosen word, write a brief problem using the word. Then switch problems with a partner and practice translating each problem into a mathematical expression.**

# Develop Your Skills

Sometimes a problem requires multiple steps, including more than one mathematical operation, in order to solve it. When this happens, there is an order that needs to be followed. You must complete each mathematical step in a particular order to ensure that your result is correct.

## Order of Operations

Take a look at the two number sentences below.

$$4 + 3 \times 6 = 42 \qquad\qquad 4 + 3 \times 6 = 22$$

You probably noticed that even though the numbers and operations are the same, the answers are different. How is this possible? The answers are different because the operations were performed in a different order. The first example was solved from left to right, which means that $4 + 3$ was first added, and then the sum (7) was multiplied by 6 to get 42. In the second example, the multiplication ($3 \times 6$) was performed first and then the product (18) was added to 4 to get 22.

The second example is the correct answer because the **order of operations** was followed. The order of operations tells you which steps must be performed first, second, and so on when operating with numbers.

1. Do what is in parentheses first.

2. Then multiply and/or divide from left to right.

3. Finally, add and/or subtract from left to right.

**Read the scenario below. Then answer the questions that follow.**

You are driving the football team in a school bus to their game on Friday night. You figure it will take 1.5 hours to travel the highway if you drive an average speed of 50 miles per hour. After you exit the highway, the school is 3.2 miles farther. How far away is the game?

1. What are the key words in this problem?

2. What operations would you use to solve the problem?

3. Write an expression that represents the distance to the game.

## Choose the Operations

Take a look at the examples on the next page. There are two operations used in each example. What operations would you use to solve the problems? How do you solve the problems?

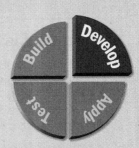

**Example:**

Before the store opened in the morning, you stocked three displays of oranges for a special sale in the produce department. At the end of the day you need to find out how many oranges were sold. How would you find the number of oranges that were sold during the day? In what order would you complete the mathematical operations? *The two operations you would use are addition and subtraction. You would add the oranges that are left at the end of the day and subtract that total from the number of oranges you put in the displays in the morning.*

**Example:**

On an assembly line, Marco assembles 320 toys in an 8-hour day. Greta assembles 304 toys in an 8-hour day. How would you find the difference in the number of toys each person can assemble in one hour? *You need to divide to find the number of toys each person assembled in one hour and subtract each quotient to find the difference. $(320 \div 8) - (304 \div 8) = 40 - 38 = 2$. Marco assembles 2 more toys each hour than Greta.*

> **Workplace Tip**
>
> Read the question carefully. Notice that the number given represents the number of toys each person produced in 8 hours and the question ask you to find the difference in production for only one hour.

**In Real Life**  **Overtime Earnings**

You worked 50 hours last week driving a forklift in the warehouse. You earned $12 per hour for the first 40 hours. For any overtime, you earn $1\frac{1}{2}$ the amount of your normal hourly wage. You are writing a budget for the week and want to figure out your earnings before taxes.

 **Using the scenario above, answer the following questions.**

4. How many operations will you use to solve this problem?

5. Which operations will you use?

6. Write a mathematical expression that represents your earnings for the week before taxes.

**GOT IT?**  To solve multi-step problems, use what you have learned about translating words into mathematical expressions:

- Identify key words and use them to determine the operations you need to use.

- Use the numbers and operations to write an expression.

- Find the value of the expression using order of operations.

**Answer Key**

1. hours, miles per hour, farther

2. multiplication and addition

3. $(50 \times 1.5) + 3.2$

4. two

5. multiplication and addition

6. $40(12) + 1\frac{1}{2}(12)(10) = \$660$

# Apply Your Knowledge

Many times problems in the workplace involve more than one step to solve. Make sure you follow the problem-solving steps you have learned.

**As you read the following scenarios, think about what you have learned in this lesson about mathematical expressions and order of operations. Select the correct response for each question.**

1.  You work in a mailroom as a mail sorter. On a typical day, you can sort 120 pieces of mail and 8 packages each hour. If you work an 8-hour shift, not including breaks, what is the total number of items you can sort for the whole day?

    A.    16

    B.    136

    C.    896

    D.  1,024

2.  Madeline is preparing a meal for 300 guests at a catering event. Each guest gets three-eighths pound of chicken breast as part of their meal. She wants to prepare an additional 5 pounds of chicken in case there are extra people. How many pounds of chicken will she need to buy?

    A.      50 lb

    B.    $112\frac{1}{2}$ lb

    C.    $117\frac{1}{2}$ lb

    D.  1,800 lb

3.  Manuela manages a hardware store. She is responsible for all the duties of opening and closing the store. At the end of the day, she has to count the cash drawer to record the total for cash sales. She counts thirty-two $20s, fifty-seven $10s and thirty-six $5s. How much money does she have in all?

    A.    $1,390

    B.    $4,375

    C.    $65,709

    D.  $142,844

**4.** You have a delivery route you drive once per week. When you left the depot, your odometer read 75,350 miles. At the end of the route, it read 75,625 miles. If your drive time was 5.5 hours, which expression could you use to find your average speed? (Hint: rate = distance/time)

**A.** 75,350 ÷ 5.5

**B.** 75,625 ÷ 5.5

**C.** (75,625 − 75,350) ÷ 5.5

**D.** (75,625 + 75,350) ÷ 5.5

---

## In Real Life  Put Your Skills to Work!

You have just been offered a job as a sales agent at an advertising agency. You would be working 35 hours a week and earning $12.50 per hour plus a $50.00 sales bonus if you meet your quota.

You are currently working at another advertising agency where you earn $12.00 per hour. However, you are working 40 hours a week. You receive a $45.00 sales bonus if you meet your quota. You are trying to decide which job will allow you to earn more money.

 **Think about the problem you are facing and put your skills to work! Assume that you will make your sales quota and earn the bonus each week. What is the difference in pay per week for the two jobs? If you are only concerned about which job will pay more, which job should you choose?**

**Workplace Tip**

When determining which job to choose, did you:

- Identify key words and terms?
- Use them to figure out which operations to use?
- Write expressions to represent each situation?
- Follow the order of operations?

## Think About It!

**Have you encountered problems in the workplace that had to be solved in a particular order?**

**Why is it important to follow problem-solving steps and do mathematical operations in a particular order?**

There are different strategies you can use when solving math problems that involve multiple steps. Always take your time and read the problem carefully. Then identify the key words in the problem to determine what numbers and operations need to be used. Write an expression using the information and translating the key terms in the problem. Be sure to follow the order of operations and also the steps for problem solving that you have learned throughout this chapter.

**Answer Key**

1. D
2. C
3. A
4. C

# Test Your WRC Skills

**Solving mathematical problems with multiple steps requires that you use a variety of strategies. Read the following situations. Select which answer you think is the correct response.**

1. You are working on a loading dock. You earn $8.50 per hour. In addition, you earn $3.00 for every crate that you can load on the truck. One day, you load 10 crates in the 6 hours you work. What are your total earnings for the day?

   | | | |
   |---|---|---|
   | **A.** | ○ | $21 |
   | **B.** | ○ | $51 |
   | **C.** | ○ | $81 |
   | **D.** | ○ | $153 |

2. You are a forklift operator who moves merchandise in a warehouse. Your forklift has a weight capacity of 3,000 pounds. You have to move two boxes that weigh 750 pounds apiece and four smaller boxes that weigh 350 pounds apiece. What is the total weight of the boxes?

   | | | |
   |---|---|---|
   | **A.** | ○ | 1,100 lb |
   | **B.** | ○ | 2,900 lb |
   | **C.** | ○ | 100 lb |
   | **D.** | ○ | 1,458 lb |

3. As a cashier, you know that the total amount of sales you have each day is the sum of the cash in your drawer, the checks received, and credit transactions minus the cash you started the day with as change in your drawer. At the end of the day, you have $1,245 in cash, $654 in checks, and $3,891 in credit transactions. If you started with $125 cash in your drawer, what were your total sales at the end of the day?

   | | | |
   |---|---|---|
   | **A.** | ○ | $5,790 |
   | **B.** | ○ | $5,915 |
   | **C.** | ○ | $5,011 |
   | **D.** | ○ | $5,665 |

4. As a construction worker, you are asked by your supervisor to cut 1.25-foot pieces from an 8-foot board and a 10-foot board. How many total pieces will you be able to cut from the two boards?

   | | | |
   |---|---|---|
   | **A.** | ○ | 2 |
   | **B.** | ○ | 14 |
   | **C.** | ○ | 18 |
   | **D.** | ○ | 48 |

**5.** You are a factory worker who assembles special computer chips. On a typical day, you can assemble 15 chips. At the end of the 5-day work week, you realize that you have assembled 7 fewer chips than you normally assemble in a week. How many chips did you assemble?

| A. | ○ | 68 |
|----|---|----|
| B. | ○ | 75 |
| C. | ○ | 82 |
| D. | ○ | 100 |

**6.** For every sale that Bernard makes, he earns a $20 commission. In order to be considered as the Employee of the Month, he must make at least $1,200 in commission that month. If in the first two weeks he earns $580 in commission, how many sales does he need to make the rest of the month in order to be considered Employee of the Month?

| A. | ○ | 89 |
|----|---|----|
| B. | ○ | 60 |
| C. | ○ | 31 |
| D. | ○ | 20 |

**7.** The company you work for has $5,000 set aside for holiday bonuses. It is your job to figure out how much each employee gets. Your boss asks you to split the money evenly among all employees after subtracting $250 from the total to cover the cost of the holiday party. If there are 10 employees, how much will each employee receive?

| A. | ○ | $525 |
|----|---|------|
| B. | ○ | $475 |
| C. | ○ | $500 |
| D. | ○ | $250 |

**Check your answers on page 148.**

# Skills for the Workplace

## Determine the Reasonableness of an Answer

When you solve math problems at work, you may have cash registers or calculators that can help you calculate. No matter how you solve a problem, it is important that you be able to determine whether the answer is reasonable.

Estimating can help you to determine whether an answer is reasonable. It can also be used when you do not need an exact answer. An **estimate** is a rough calculation or approximation.

One of the most common ways to estimate is to **round** numbers. Remember, when rounding you look at the number to the right of the place to which you are rounding. For example, if you want to round 243 to the hundreds place, you would use the 4 to determine whether to round up or round down. If the number is 5 or greater, round up. If the number is less than 5, round down.

Read problems carefully to determine whether an exact answer is needed. Even if an exact answer is required, finding an estimate can help you determine whether your exact answer is reasonable or not.

### Workplace Scenario

You are working in a child care center. The children are placed in different rooms depending on their age. The table below shows each age group. It also shows the monthly cost for child care.

| Age Group | Monthly Cost (Full-Time Care) |
|---|---|
| Infants (up to 12 months old) | $679 |
| 1–3 years old | $649 |
| 4–5 years old | $535 |
| 6 years old and up | $285 |

A parent asks you what the total yearly cost would be for her 2-year-old son and 4-year-old daughter.

- Does this problem require an estimate or an exact answer? *an exact answer*

- What is the total cost of day care for this parent's children? *$14,208*

- How could you estimate the answer to check that your answer was reasonable? *You could round the costs before multiplying. If you round each cost to the nearest hundred you would find ($600 × 12) + ($500 × 12) = $13,200. Since this is close to your exact answer of $14,208, you can judge your answer to be reasonable.*

# Workplace Practice

You are working as a clerk at a furniture rental company. A customer calls you with a list of items he would like to rent and asks you to give him an estimate to the nearest hundred dollars on the total cost to rent the items.

| Item | Rental Cost (Per Month) | Number of Item Needed |
|------|-------------------------|------------------------|
| Desk chair | $39.95 | 5 |
| Bookshelf | $25.19 | 2 |
| Desk | $55.89 | 3 |
| Filing cabinet – 4-drawer | $14.14 | 6 |
| Filing cabinet – 4-drawer lateral file | $27.50 | 2 |

- Does this problem require an estimate or an exact answer? *an estimate*

- What is the first step you would take to solve the problem using the information above? *Round each cost.*

- What operations would you use to solve the problem? *multiplication and addition*

## It's Your Turn!

1. You are purchasing carpentry supplies for your company. Your cart has 4 1-pint bottles of finishing wax that each cost $10.99, 10 pairs of wrap-around hinges at $8.29 per pair, and an orbital hand sander that costs $172.89. You estimate that your total bill will come to $420.00. Is your estimate reasonable?

2. You earn $13.50 per hour as a library assistant and you work 40 hours per week. You estimate that your weekly paycheck before taxes should come to $520.00. Is your estimate greater or less than the exact amount of your paycheck before taxes?

3. You are a bus driver. One of the schools that contracts with your company orders additional service for a school field trip. There are 126 children and 15 adults going on the field trip. Each bus seats a maximum of 40 students and 4 adults. You estimate that the school will need to charter 3 buses. Does your estimate provide a sufficient number of buses?

4. Look back at the second Workplace Practice example above. What is a reasonable answer for the estimate that the customer has requested?

**Answer Key**

**1.** No. If you rounded the cost of each item to the nearest whole number, your estimate should have been about $297.

**2.** less; Your exact paycheck before taxes will be $540.00.

**3.** No. You rounded down, so your estimate is less than the number of buses needed.

**4.** Estimates may vary; $600.00

# Chapter 1 Assessment

**Read each problem and choose the best answer.**

1. You work in the stockroom of a grocery store. You receive a delivery of 30 boxes of chicken that weigh 15 pounds each. Each box contains breasts, thighs and drumsticks. What information is not needed in order to find the total weight delivered?

| | | |
|---|---|---|
| A. | ○ | the weight of the boxes |
| B. | ○ | the number of boxes |
| C. | ○ | what is in the boxes |
| D. | ○ | the unit of weight used |

2. Ahmad works as an office furniture salesman. One of his clients places an order for 30 desks that cost $420 each. How much will this order cost?

| | | |
|---|---|---|
| A. | ○ | $14 |
| B. | ○ | $390 |
| C. | ○ | $450 |
| D. | ○ | $12,600 |

3. Your boss asks you to find co-workers who want to attend a leadership seminar next month. He informs you that you have a $1,200 budget to spend on registration. The registration fee is $80 per person. Which expression would you use to determine how many people from your office can go to the seminar?

| | | |
|---|---|---|
| A. | ○ | 1,200 ÷ 80 |
| B. | ○ | 80 ÷ 1,200 |
| C. | ○ | 1,200 − 80 |
| D. | ○ | 80 × 1,200 |

4. You are a tow truck driver and you get paid $2 for every mile that you drive plus a flat rate of $20 per vehicle towed. If on a given day you drove 130 miles and you towed 5 cars, how much money would you earn?

| | | |
|---|---|---|
| A. | ○ | $100 |
| B. | ○ | $260 |
| C. | ○ | $360 |
| D. | ○ | $650 |

5. As a medical assistant, your job requires you to spend equal amounts of time throughout your day with every patient that you see. You work a 12-hour shift. What information do you need to determine how much time you should spend with each patient?

| A. | ○ | what room the patient is in |
| B. | ○ | how ill the patient is |
| C. | ○ | how many patients you are caring for |
| D. | ○ | how many doctors are on duty |

6. As an assistant chef, you are able to make around 30 salads per hour. If the restaurant averages 50 orders for salads per hour, about how many salads must someone else in the kitchen make every hour to keep up with all of the orders?

| A. | ○ | 20 |
| B. | ○ | 30 |
| C. | ○ | 40 |
| D. | ○ | 80 |

7. If you have to travel 330 miles in 6 hours, which expression would you use to find the average speed you must maintain in order to arrive at your destination in time?

| A. | ○ | $330 \times 6$ |
| B. | ○ | $\dfrac{330}{6}$ |
| C. | ○ | $330 - 6$ |
| D. | ○ | $330 + 6$ |

8. You pack boxes of potato chips and pretzels at a snack factory. Each box of potato chips contains 8 bags and each box of pretzels contains 10 bags. You pack 30 boxes of chips and 40 boxes of pretzels in one day. How many bags of chips and pretzels have you packed?

| A. | ○ | 70 |
| B. | ○ | 88 |
| C. | ○ | 640 |
| D. | ○ | 96,000 |

For more Chapter 1 assessment questions, please visit www.mysteckvaughn.com/WORK

**Check your answers on page 149.**

# 2 Number Operations

You likely use numbers every day. Activities such as making purchases, paying bills, and figuring out your schedule all involve using math skills. In this chapter, you will practice working with money, including making change and reconciling budgets. You will also solve problems that involve fractions, decimals, and percents in real-life situations.

# Work with Currency

## Essential Tasks

**Use decimals** in the form of monetary values

**Create simple expressions** or formulas **from real-life situations** or from tables

**Apply order of operations** in simple multi-step problems

## Build on What You Know

Of all the different ways you use math every day, working with money is probably the most common and the one with which you are the most familiar. Think about how you used money today or over the past few days. Perhaps you bought food or an item of clothing. Maybe you checked the balance on your bank account or paid a bill. Even if you do not use bills and coins but pay with a check, debit, or credit card, you are still using money.

It is essential in the workplace to be able to work with money. Why is it so important? Money assigns value to the products and services that companies provide. In most jobs, you will have to deal with money. You may be expected to order supplies and receive or make payments to customers and other vendors and suppliers. It is also important that you understand how to work with budgets.

In this lesson, you will learn how to solve problems involving money, including adding, subtracting, multiplying, and dividing with decimal forms of money. When solving these problems, you should follow the steps for problem solving that you learned in the last chapter. You should always read the problem carefully to identify the relevant facts and the question that is being asked. Look for key words that indicate the operations involved.

### In Real Life    What Is the Total Cost?

You are working in the sales department at A.J.'s Tire Repair Shop. A customer calls to get a price on replacing all 4 tires on his car. When you look up the price for the tire for his vehicle, it is listed as $45.75 per tire, including installation.

  **With a classmate, discuss the following questions. Share your ideas with the class.**

1. What are the important facts in this problem?

2. What is the problem you are trying to solve?

3. Which operation(s) would you use to find the price of the 4 tires?

### Workplace Tip

The word "per" is important in word problems. It can often indicate that you will need to multiply or divide.

**Teacher Reminder**

Review the teacher lesson at www.mysteckvaughn.com/WORK

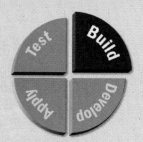

When solving problems that involve money, it is important to understand the different units of currency used in order to make correct change. It is also necessary to identify the correct operation(s) and be able to work with decimals.

## Currency: Bills and Coins

When you are working with money, it is important to remember the value of the different units of currency. The basic unit of U.S. currency is the dollar. Coins are used to make up the value of money when it is less than a dollar. When expressing monetary values in written form, decimals are used to represent the value of coins. The table below shows you the value of each coin.

| Coin | Value |
|---|---|
| Penny | $0.01 |
| Nickel | $0.05 |
| Dime | $0.10 |
| Quarter | $0.25 |
| 50-Cent Piece | $0.50 |

In addition to coins, you likely deal with $1, $5, $10, and $20 bills on a regular basis. You may also see bills worth $50 and $100.

## Operating with Decimals

Because money involves decimals, it is important to remember what you know about mathematical operations involving decimals:

- When you add or subtract numbers that include decimals, you must line up the decimal points before adding or subtracting.
- When you multiply numbers that include decimals, remember that the product must have the same number of decimal places (numbers to the right of the decimal point) as the total number of decimal places in the numbers you are multiplying.
- When you divide numbers with decimals, be sure to make the divisor a whole number, if necessary, and move the decimal point in the dividend the same number of places (adding placeholder zeros if necessary). Then place the decimal point in the appropriate place in the quotient.

 **With a classmate, discuss the following questions. Share your ideas with the class.**

 **4.** Do you usually deal with money in cash or use a credit or debit card? What are the differences between the two?

# Develop Your Skills

In the workplace, money is used to buy and sell products and services and to pay employees. Companies may also pay off debt, invest in items such as computers, or keep the money as profit.

In what ways do you think you will interact with money when doing your job? Will you need to determine a customer's bill, receive the payment, and make change for the customer? Will you need to purchase supplies? Will you be responsible for managing or maintaining some kind of budget?

 **With a classmate, discuss the following question. Share your ideas with the class.**

1. Have you ever made a personal budget or a budget for work?

## Bills Paid, Change Received

You probably often pay for products or services in cash. What happens when you do not have the exact change? You pay the bill with an amount that is greater than what you owe, and then you receive change. In order to determine the amount of change you will receive, the amount owed is subtracted from the amount received. Once the amount of change is figured, that amount can often be paid in more than one way.

You are working at the concession stand at a movie theater. A customer orders a large popcorn and drink combo for $8.75 and a box of candy for $2.50. The customer gives you $20.00 to pay for his purchases.

 **Using the scenario above, answer the following questions.**

2. What operations are involved in solving the problem?

3. How much change should you give the customer?

4. Is there more than one combination of bills and coins that you could give the customer and still provide the correct change? What combination would use the fewest bills and coins?

### Workplace Tip

If possible, it is good to make change with the largest denominations possible. So, if the change is $8.75, you would not give the customer 875 pennies.

## Working with a Budget

You may have worked with a budget before when dealing with your personal finances. A **budget** is an amount of money that is allocated for a particular purpose. For example, if you earn $1,875 per month after taxes, you may make a budget to figure out how you can pay your bills, save some money, and have some left over to spend on things that you want.

Businesses use budgets in much the same way. They set aside money for things such as payroll, supplies such as paper and computers, and other items specific to the type of work they do. Many businesses also budget for expenses like advertising and travel for conferences and client meetings.

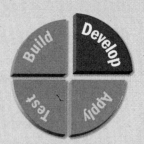

Another reason that individuals and businesses make budgets is to monitor spending. Sometimes more money is spent on an item or category than was originally planned for. In a budget, this is indicated by a negative number.

When you check to see you are within or over the amounts allocated in a budget, it is called reconciling the budget. To **reconcile** the budget, subtract the amount spent from the amount budgeted. If the amount spent is less than the amount budgeted, the number will be positive. If the amount spent is more than the amount budgeted, the number will be negative.

**Example:**

You are an administrative assistant at a bookbinding company. Your boss asks you to reconcile the budget for supplies. You make the calculations and submit the figures in the spreadsheet shown below.

| Item/Supply | Amount Budgeted | Amount Spent | Balance |
|---|---|---|---|
| Binder board (different sizes) | $100.00 | $103.75 | −$3.75 |
| | $450.00 | $443.75 | $6.25 |
| Board shear | $3,500.00 | $3,695.00 | −$195.00 |
| Glue | $200.00 | $204.85 | −$4.85 |
| Glue brushes | $225.00 | $210.00 | $15.00 |
| Cotton tape | $300.00 | $297.00 | $3.00 |
| Totals | $4,775.00 | $4,954.35 | −$179.35 |

 **Using the scenario above, answer the following questions.**

**5.** Which items were within budget?

**6.** Which items were over budget?

**7.** What was the overall balance on the budget? What does it mean?

**GOT IT?** **In order to solve problems working with money and budgets, remember to:**

• Use the rules for operating with decimals, and double-check to be sure that you have placed the decimal point in the correct place.

• Subtract the amount owed from the amount paid, and determine the correct amounts of bills and coins to use when making change.

• Subtract the amount spent from the amount budgeted, and determine if the balance is positive or negative to reconcile budgets.

**Answer Key**

**2** addition and subtraction

**3.** $8.75

**4.** Yes, there is more than one combination. The combination with the fewest bills and coins is one $5 bill, three $1 bills, and three quarters.

**5.** one size of binder board, glue brushes, and cotton tape

**6.** the other size of binder board, board shear, and glue

**7.** The overall balance is −$179.35. It means that the company spent $179.35 more on supplies than they had originally budgeted.

# Apply Your Knowledge

In order to solve real-world problems involving money, you must first read the problem carefully to determine what the problem requires you to do. Be sure to identify all operations necessary to solve the problem.

**As you read the following scenarios, think about what the problem is asking you to do. Select the correct response for each question.**

1. You have received a delivery of 10 crates containing boxes of crackers. Each crate contains 18 boxes of crackers. If you must pay $1.25 per box of crackers, what do you owe for the crackers?

   A. $12.50

   B. $22.50

   C. $29.25

   D. $225.00

2. You are working the cash register in a hardware store. A customer makes a purchase that costs $19.37, including tax. She pays with a $20 bill. What combination of coins represents the correct change?

   A. one quarter, one dime, and three pennies

   B. one quarter, two dimes, and three pennies

   C. two quarters, one dime, and three pennies

   D. two quarters, two dimes, and three pennies

3. You are reconciling your monthly budget for the floral design shop where you work. The budget figures are shown below. Which items are within the amount budgeted for the month?

| Item/Supply | Amount Budgeted | Amount Spent | Balance |
| --- | --- | --- | --- |
| Floral foam | $1,200.00 | $1,240.00 | –$40.00 |
| Vases | $300.00 | $249.50 | $50.50 |
| Floral wire | $200.00 | $220.80 | –$20.80 |
| Floral tape/stem wrap | $275.00 | $262.25 | $12.75 |
| Ribbon | $100.00 | $91.80 | $8.20 |

   A. floral foam, floral wire, and ribbon

   B. floral foam and floral wire

   C. vases, floral tape/stem wrap, and ribbon

   D. All items were within budget.

4. You work for an automotive-parts supply company. You received payments from customers in the amounts of $432.63, $712.38, and $906.23. From this money, you paid your delivery person $122.50. How much money is left?

   A. $2,173.74

   B. $1,928.74

   C. $1,063.48

   D. $116.28

## In Real Life   Put Your Skills to Work!

You are visiting a school's athletic department to sell them equipment. They have a budget of $350.00 to spend on equipment. You sell them some soccer balls for a total of $199.80, field paint for $29.95, and weight equipment for $48.75. They pay you $300.00 cash. Then the athletic director tells you that he still needs to purchase 10 basketballs. How much money is left in his budget? If your company sells basketballs for $11.49, how many basketballs can the athletic director afford to buy without going over his budget?

 **Think about the problem you are facing and put your skills to work! What operations do you need to use to solve this problem? Which skills that you have learned about in this lesson will you use to solve the problem?**

## Workplace Tip

When making your decision, did you:

- Determine which operations you needed to use to solve?
- Follow the rules for operating with decimals?
- Find the difference between what was owed and what was paid?
- Reconcile the budget to determine how much the athletic director had left to spend without going over budget?

## Think About It!

**How have you worked with money in your daily life and at work?**

**Have you used devices such as a cash register or calculator when working with money? Why is it important to know how to work with money even when you have these devices to help you do the calculations?**

When solving problems involving money, apply the same problem-solving steps you learned in the previous chapter. Read the problem to determine what the question is asking and which operations you will use. If decimal amounts of money are involved, follow the rules for operating with decimals. At work, you may find that there are devices such as cash registers and calculators that can help you. However, these devices may not always be available. It is important to be able to determine that an answer, whether you've calculated it by hand or with a device, is reasonable and makes sense.

**Answer Key**

1 D

2. C

3. C

4. B

# Test Your WRC Skills

**Solving problems involving money requires understanding how to work with different bills and coins and computing with decimals. Read the following situations. Select which answer you think is the correct response.**

1. You have made three purchases this morning to replenish supplies for the office. You spent $86.63 for paper, $26.87 for clips of various sizes, and $43.50 for file folders. What was the total amount you spent this morning?

| | | |
|---|---|---|
| A. ○ | $0.000157 |
| B. ○ | $113.50 |
| C. ○ | $157.00 |
| D. ○ | $15,700.00 |

2. You earn $14.55 per hour working on an assembly line. You work four 10-hour shifts each week. How much money do you earn in one day?

| | | |
|---|---|---|
| A. ○ | $14.55 |
| B. ○ | $58.20 |
| C. ○ | $145.50 |
| D. ○ | $582.00 |

3. You sell breakfast items at a shop in the airport. The price of each of the items you sell is shown in the table below. A customer orders a breakfast sandwich, a fruit smoothie, and a coffee. What is the cost of the breakfast, not including taxes?

| Item | Price |
|---|---|
| Breakfast Sandwich | $4.99 |
| Fruit Danish | $2.25 |
| Fruit Smoothie | $3.49 |
| Coffee | $1.99 |
| Juice | $2.49 |

| | | |
|---|---|---|
| A. ○ | $6.98 |
| B. ○ | $10.47 |
| C. ○ | $10.97 |
| D. ○ | $15.21 |

4. You are the manager at A-Plus Cellular. The most popular phone you sell retails for $129.49. Today, you sold 10 of these phones. With every phone, you also sold a $30.00 accessories package. What are your total sales today?

| A. | ○ | $159.49 |
| B. | ○ | $1,294.90 |
| C. | ○ | $994.90 |
| D. | ○ | $1,594.90 |

5. A customer buys $9.34 worth of merchandise. He pays with a $10 bill. Which combination of coins represents the correct change he should receive?

| A. | ○ | two quarters, one dime, one nickel, and one penny |
| B. | ○ | two quarters, two dimes, one nickel, and one penny |
| C. | ○ | three quarters, one dime, one nickel, and one penny |
| D. | ○ | three quarters, two dimes, one nickel, and one penny |

6. You are on a business trip attending a convention to demonstrate your company's products. Your budget for travel expenses is $450.00. So far, you have spent $126.60 on gasoline, $226.37 on meals with clients, and $65.00 for one night in a hotel. How much money do you have left to spend?

| A. | ○ | $32.03 |
| B. | ○ | $97.03 |
| C. | ○ | $417.97 |
| D. | ○ | $867.97 |

7. You pay a cleaning-supply vendor in cash to receive a discount. The bill, after your discount is applied, comes to $123.76. You give the vendor $125.00. Which of the following represents the correct amount of change you should receive?

| A. | ○ | two dollars, one quarter, and one penny |
| B. | ○ | two dollars, two dimes, and four pennies |
| C. | ○ | one dollar, one quarter, and one penny |
| D. | ○ | one dollar, two dimes, and four pennies |

Check your answers on page 150.

# Understand Percents

## Build on What You Know

You have likely seen and used percents many times in your life. Percents are often used to give test scores, indicate a marked-down price in a store, or to give an interest rate on a savings or checking account.

Some of the ways that businesses use percents are:

- to determine what to charge for products and services,
- to track sales and inventory,
- to find staffing and employee productivity,
- to allocate money and other resources and track expenses,
- and to monitor work processes and the status of employee tasks.

In this lesson, you will learn how to work with percents in workplace situations. Understanding the meaning of percents and knowing how to work with them are important skills for the workplace and in everyday life.

### In Real Life    How Do You Use Percents?

William manages a catering business. He understands that to keep things running smoothly and to make a profit, he must keep food costs down, maintain the equipment, and pay the employees fairly.

William must keep all of these factors in mind when determining what to charge a customer. He figures that for each event, he needs to keep each expense at the percent shown in the table below.

| Food | 25% |
| --- | --- |
| Labor | 15% |
| Equipment maintenance | 5% |

 **Discuss the scenario with your classmates. Share your ideas with the class.**

1. Why are percents important in William's position as a manager?

2. In what ways can William affect the profit that the company makes?

3. If the amount left after he pays his expenses is profit, what percent of the amount he charges the customer is profit?

# Percents, Fractions, and Decimals

Remember that a **ratio** compares two amounts. For example, suppose you learn that 2 out of every 5 people read the newspaper on Sunday. The ratio of people who read the newspaper to the total number of people is $\frac{2}{5}$.

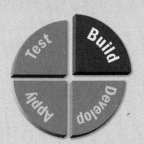

A **percent** is a ratio that tells you how many out of 100. *Percent* means "per 100." A percent is similar to a fraction in that it represents the part of a whole where the whole (or denominator) is always 100. To write a percent as a fraction, you put the percent in the numerator (part) of the fraction and 100 in the denominator (whole).

For example, suppose you were responsible for inspecting items as they come off an assembly line. In one hour, you inspect 100 items. Out of those 100 items, 75 are approved. This means 75% of the items passed inspection. As a fraction, 75% would be written as $\frac{75}{100}$. You can then reduce the fraction to $\frac{3}{4}$. This means 3 out of every 4 items passed inspection.

To rewrite a fraction as a percent, first rewrite the fraction as a decimal. Then move the decimal point two places to the right and add the percent symbol (%): $\frac{3}{4} = 0.75 = 75\%$.

Percents can also be expressed, or rewritten, as decimals. In order to write a percent as a decimal, simply move the decimal point two places to the left and remove the percent symbol: 75% = 0.75.

When you solve math problems with percents, you will usually need to convert the percent to a fraction or a decimal before you solve. You may also need to convert your answer back to a percent. The following statements summarize how to convert between fractions, decimals, and percents.

1. **Fraction to Decimal** – Divide the numerator by the denominator.

2. **Fraction to Percent** – Convert to a decimal, then move the decimal point two places to the right, and add the percent symbol (%).

3. **Decimal to Fraction** – Convert to a percent, write as a fraction over 100, and reduce.

4. **Decimal to Percent** – Move the decimal point two places to the right and add the percent symbol (%).

5. **Percent to Decimal** – Move the decimal point two places to the left and remove the percent symbol (%).

6. **Percent to Fraction** – Write the percent as a fraction over 100 and then reduce.

 **Ask yourself the following question. Share your ideas with the class.**

4. Think of a situation where you saw or worked with a percent. What was the percent? What did it mean?

# Develop Your Skills

When solving problems involving percents, the first step is to understand what the percent represents. Ask yourself:

- What is the question asking?
- What is this percent as a fraction or decimal?
- What does this percent mean?

**Workplace Tip**

In many jobs you will be required to manage a budget. Percents work nicely for budgets because you want to plan the use of 100% of the money allotted. Understanding percents is important when working with a budget.

## What Is the Question Asking?

You are planning a company picnic, and you have a budget of $500. The money assigned to each category is shown in the table below.

| Item | Cost |
| --- | --- |
| Food and Drinks | $300 |
| Plates, Cups, and Napkins | $50 |
| Decorations | $50 |
| Park Pavilion Rental | $100 |

 **Use the information above to answer the following questions.**

1. What are the parts in this situation?

2. What is the whole?

3. How could you find the percent of your budget that you are spending on food and drinks?

## Solving Problems with Percents

Problems involving percents usually ask you to find either the part, the whole, or the percent. The relationship between these different elements can be represented by an equation: Percent × Whole = Part.

You can use this equation to solve percent problems. Read the problem carefully to identify which pieces of information you have and which you are being asked to find. Then substitute what you know into the equation and use the equation to solve. You will need to change percents to decimals or fractions before calculating.

**Example:**

Tressa is a waitress at a local diner. On a particular night, she earns $25 per hour, including tips. Her hourly wage, not including tips, is 20% of her hourly earnings. What is her hourly wage before tips? *Identify what you know: the whole is $25. Her hourly wages are 20% of the whole. You need to find the part. Multiply: 0.2 × 25 = 5. She earns $5 per hour before tips.*

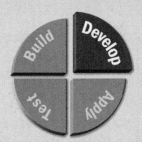

**Example:**

As a hospital orderly, you are responsible for taking patients' vital signs when you start your shift. You have taken the vital signs of 18 patients, or 75% of your patients so far. How many patients' vital signs do you check? *Identify what you know: the part is 18 patients. This is 75% of the whole. You need to find the whole. Divide: $18 \div 0.75$ (or $\frac{3}{4}$) = 24. You are responsible for checking the vital signs of 24 patients.*

**Example:**

Jonathan works as a custodian. He adds 8 ounces of concentrated floor cleaner to 72 ounces of water to make a cleaning solution. What percent of the cleaning solution is concentrated floor cleaner? *Identify what you know: the part is 8 ounces. The whole is 8 ounces + 72 ounces, or 80 ounces. Divide: $8 \div 80 = 0.1$. Convert the decimal to a percent: $0.1 = 10\%$. The cleaning solution is 10% concentrated floor clearer.*

---

**In Real Life**  **More Percents!**

You are mowing lawns for a landscaping company. At the beginning of the week you are given a list of 125 lawns you must mow by the end of the week. You mow 25 lawns on Monday, 35 lawns on Tuesday, 30 lawns on Wednesday, 20 lawns on Thursday, and 15 lawns on Friday. What percent of the lawns did you mow on Monday?

 **Answer the following questions.**

4. What are the part and the whole for the question being asked?

5. What percent of lawns did you mow on Monday?

6. How could you figure out the percent of the lawns you mowed on Monday, Tuesday, and Wednesday?

---

**GOT IT?**  **When solving problems involving percents, remember to follow these steps:**

- Identify what you know: are you given the part? the whole? the percent?

- Using the percent equation, substitute the information that you know into the equation.

- Convert the percent to a fraction or a decimal.

- Complete your calculations. If you are finding a percent, be sure to convert your answer to a percent.

**Answer Key**

**1.** The parts are 300, 50, 50, and 100.

**2.** 500

**3.** Divide the part (300) by the whole (500) and change the answer to a percent.

**4.** The part is 25 lawns and the whole is 125 lawns.

**5.** 20%

**6.** Add the number of lawns you mowed on those three days together. Use the sum as the part and the week's total as the whole. Divide the part by the whole and then convert your answer to a percent.

# Apply Your Knowledge

As you look at the following questions, think about the problem-solving strategies you have learned. Remember the information that you need to identify and the steps you used to solve percent problems.

**Read each percent problem and answer the three key questions below. Then select the correct response for each question.**

1. You are a sales representative for medical supplies. In order to meet your sales quota for the week, you must sell $500 worth of supplies. On Tuesday, you make $200 in sales. What percent of your weekly sales goal did you sell on Tuesday?

   • What pieces of information do you know?
   • What information is the question asking you to find?
   • Do you need to convert your answer, and if so, how will you convert?

   **A.**  4%

   **B.**  20%

   **C.**  40%

   **D.** 400%

2. You are working as an administrative assistant. Your boss asks you to use 25% of the office-supply budget to buy copy paper, legal pads, and pens. If the total office-supply budget is $500, how much money do you have to spend on the supplies your boss asked you to purchase?

   • What pieces of information do you know?
   • What information is the question asking you to find?
   • How do you find that information?

   **A.**  $25

   **B.**  $50

   **C.**  $125

   **D.**  $500

## In Real Life — Put Your Skills to Work!

You are an assistant in the accounting department of a company. You are asked to manage and track each department's budget using figures given to you by the department heads. The sales department has a monthly budget of $25,000. When you were calculating the latest figures, you found that the sales department was 15% over budget for the month.

**Think about the problem you are facing and put your skills to work! How would you determine the amount of money that the sales department is over budget? What information would you need in order to make suggestions to the department head about how her department could get back under budget?**

**Workplace Tip**

When thinking of ways you use percents in the workplace, think about:

- what you know and what you are trying to find.
- how you can use what you know to find the piece of information you need.
- how to convert percents to decimals and fractions and back again.

## Think About It!

What are some ways you use percents in daily life and in the workplace?

Describe some situations in the workplace where percents are used.

When dealing with percent problems, what do you need to recognize first?

Percents are often used when describing relationships that can be expressed as "how much per 100." For example, if you have a savings account that earns 2% interest, that means that for every $100 you keep in the account, you will earn $2 in interest.

In this lesson, you learned how to use percents to solve problems. The first thing you need to recognize with percent problems is what the question is asking. Does the problem ask you to find the part, the whole, or the percent? Identifying the key information in the problem, including what you need to find, is very important when solving problems involving percents.

# Test Your WRC Skills

**Read each percent problem. Select which answer you think is the correct response.**

**1.** Sanjay gets paid $6 commission for every $50 worth of merchandise he sells at a department store. What percent of sales is his commission?

| | | |
|---|---|---|
| **A.** | ○ | 0.12% |
| **B.** | ○ | 6% |
| **C.** | ○ | 12% |
| **D.** | ○ | 120% |

**2.** Pedro was given $400 to spend on a business luncheon. The table below shows how he spent the money. What percent of the money did he spend on decorations?

| Item | Money Spent |
|---|---|
| Food | $250 |
| Drinks | $25 |
| Decorations | $50 |
| Room rental fee | $75 |

| | | |
|---|---|---|
| **A.** | ○ | 12.5% |
| **B.** | ○ | 18.75% |
| **C.** | ○ | 50% |
| **D.** | ○ | 62.5% |

**3.** Gretchen works in health care. Each week, 5% of her paycheck goes towards health insurance. If her weekly paycheck is $650.00, how much money does she pay each week for her health insurance?

| | | |
|---|---|---|
| **A.** | ○ | $5.00 |
| **B.** | ○ | $32.50 |
| **C.** | ○ | $325.00 |
| **D.** | ○ | $617.50 |

4. You are an assistant to the manager of a retail store. He wants to figure out what percent of the total sales on a given day were made in the lawn and garden department. The lawn and garden department sales were $1,500. The total sales for the retail store were $10,000. What percent of the total sales came from the lawn and garden department?

| | | |
|---|---|---|
| A. | ○ | 0.15% |
| B. | ○ | 1.5% |
| C. | ○ | 15% |
| D. | ○ | 125% |

5. New laws require restaurants to provide nutritional facts to their customers. As a manager, you need to figure out this information so that you can post it on your menu. A certain cheeseburger has 560 calories. Of that total, 210 calories come from fat. What percent of the calories are **NOT** from fat?

| | | |
|---|---|---|
| A. | ○ | 3.75% |
| B. | ○ | 6.25% |
| C. | ○ | 37.5% |
| D. | ○ | 62.5% |

6. The following chart shows the breakdown of sales for Brenda's gift shop in the month of August. What percent of total sales were from candles and gift cards?

| Item | Sales Amount |
|---|---|
| Candles | $298 |
| Decorations | $345 |
| Collectibles | $762 |
| Gift cards | $395 |

| | | |
|---|---|---|
| A. | ○ | 0.385% |
| B. | ○ | 38.5% |
| C. | ○ | 61.5% |
| D. | ○ | 260% |

Check your answers on page 151.

# Skills for the Workplace
## Make Correct Change

You probably use money every day. You may buy some coffee or pay bills. Perhaps you also work in a job that deals with money on a daily basis.

It is important both as a customer and as an employee to be able to calculate costs and determine the correct change. As a customer, you want to be sure that you receive what is owed to you. As an employee, your boss expects you to charge the customer correctly and return the correct change.

In the workplace, cash registers will often calculate the total cost of a purchase and the correct change. However, there may be times when you enter an incorrect amount, or the customer finds some additional change to give you. In these cases, and in others when electronic aids are not available, you need to know how to find and make correct change.

To do so, you need to know the total purchase price and the amount that the customer has paid. Subtract the payment from the purchase amount. This will tell you how much the customer is owed. Then figure out how to make that amount using the fewest number of bills and coins that you can. However, there may be times when you need to adjust the combination. For instance, if you owe a customer $0.50 but are out of quarters, you may give the customer five dimes.

### Workplace Scenario

You are working as a pharmacy aide. A customer picks up her prescriptions. One prescription costs $4.95 and the other costs $12.45. She also wants to purchase a toothbrush for $6.99 and some mouthwash for $5.79. She gives you two $20 bills to pay for her purchase.

- How much money has the customer given you? *$40.00*

- What is the total cost of the purchase? *$30.18*

- How much change is the customer owed? *$9.82*

- What combination of bills and coins would you give to the customer as change using the fewest number possible? *one $5 bill, four $1 bills, three quarters, one nickel, and two pennies*

### Workplace Scenario

You are working as a hostess in a diner. One of your responsibilities is to take payments from customers. A customer comes to pay his bill of $11.55. He gives you a $20 bill. The cash register is out of $5 bills and dimes.

- How much change is the customer owed? *$8.45*

- What combination of bills and coins should you give to the customer? *You are out of $5 bills, so you will need to give him eight $1 bills. You are also out of dimes, so you will need to give him one quarter and four nickels.*

## Workplace Practice

You are working as a cashier in a grocery store. A customer makes a purchase of $33.78. She gives you two $20 bills and you enter $40.00 as the payment amount. She then realizes that she has $0.03 and gives that to you as well.

- Why did the customer give you three pennies? *She gave you three pennies because the change portion of her purchase was $0.78. If she gives you $0.03, she will receive a quarter back rather than two dimes and two pennies.*

- How much change is the customer owed? *$6.25*

- What combination of bills and coins should you give to the customer? *one $5 bill, one $1 bill, and one quarter*

### Workplace Tip

Remember that you'd like to give the customer the fewest number of bills and coins when making change. However, when you are lacking some bills and coins, you need to adjust how you will make change. You should still try to give the fewest number with the bills and coins that you have.

## It's Your Turn!

1. You are working as a dog groomer. A customer brings in three dogs to be groomed. Two of the dogs are small dogs, for which you charge $45 each. The third dog is a large dog, for which you charge $98. The large dog also needs to have its hair de-matted, for which you charge an additional $8. The customer gives you two $100 bills to pay. How much change do you owe her?

2. The dry-cleaning shop where you work has the following prices posted for its services:

| Service | Cost |
|---|---|
| Same-day dry-cleaning (shirts) | $8.19 |
| Dry-cleaning (shirts) | $6.35 |
| Wash-dry-fold service (per pound) | $1.52 |

A customer drops off two shirts and requests same-day service. He also gives you 13 pounds of laundry that he would like to have washed, dried, and folded. He gives you one $20 and two $10 bills to pay. How much change do you need to give him?

3. You are working as a cashier. A customer gives you one $10 bill and one $5 bill to pay for a purchase in the amount of $11.26. Then she gives you a penny. How much change do you owe the customer, and how would you give it to her?

**Answer Key**

**1.** $4

**2.** $3.86

**3.** $3.75; You should give the customer three $1 bills and three quarters.

# Chapter 2 Assessment

**Read each problem and choose the best answer.**

**1.** Every 2 weeks, Shun takes 20% of his $850 paycheck and deposits it into a savings account. After 6 weeks, how much money has he deposited in his savings account?

| | | |
|---|---|---|
| **A.** | ○ | $170 |
| **B.** | ○ | $340 |
| **C.** | ○ | $510 |
| **D.** | ○ | $1,020 |

**2.** The table below shows the prices of items sold in a coffee shop. On Thursday the shop offers 10% off all items on the menu. What would be the total price of a medium coffee and a blueberry scone after the discount?

| Item | Original Price |
|---|---|
| Medium Coffee | $1.40 |
| Cranberry Muffin | $2.10 |
| Cappuccino | $3.25 |
| Blueberry Scone | $2.50 |

| | | |
|---|---|---|
| **A.** | ○ | $0.39 |
| **B.** | ○ | $3.51 |
| **C.** | ○ | $3.90 |
| **D.** | ○ | $4.29 |

**3.** Beth makes $10.25 an hour at a manufacturing plant. If she works 8-hour days, 6 days a week, how much money will she earn in one week, not including any overtime pay?

| | | |
|---|---|---|
| **A.** | ○ | $10.25 |
| **B.** | ○ | $82.00 |
| **C.** | ○ | $410.00 |
| **D.** | ○ | $492.00 |

4. Every month you receive a $450.00 budget for maintenance around the factory you work in. So far this month you have spent $126.89 to fix the air conditioning and $239.06 on cleaning and waxing the floors. How much money is left in the budget for maintenance this month?

| A. | ○ | $84.05 |
| B. | ○ | $210.94 |
| C. | ○ | $323.11 |
| D. | ○ | $815.95 |

5. As a medical assistant at the local hospital, you are required to check the blood pressure of 20% of the patients on the third floor and 20% of the patients on the fourth floor. If there are 20 patients on the third floor and 30 patients on the fourth floor, how many patients should you see?

| A. | ○ | 4 |
| B. | ○ | 6 |
| C. | ○ | 10 |
| D. | ○ | 50 |

6. Warren earns $12,336.24 in a 6-month period. If he is paid once a month, how much does he earn each month?

| A. | ○ | $1,028.02 |
| B. | ○ | $2,056.04 |
| C. | ○ | $4,112.08 |
| D. | ○ | $74,017.44 |

7. The table below shows the extra services you can choose from with a standard cable package that costs $46.99 per month. If you choose to add the high-definition service and the digital-video-recorder service, how much is your total cable bill per month?

| Extra Services | Price Per Month |
| --- | --- |
| Movie Channels | $6.50 |
| High Definition | $7.25 |
| Digital Video Recorder | $9.75 |

| A. | ○ | $29.99 |
| B. | ○ | $46.99 |
| C. | ○ | $63.99 |
| D. | ○ | $70.49 |

 For more Chapter 2 assessment questions, please visit www.mysteckvaughn.com/WORK

Check your answers on page 152.

# 3 Measurement and Geometry

Just about every job involves measurement in some way. Knowing how to take measurements, which units of measure to use, and how to choose the appropriate measurement tools are important workplace skills. In this chapter, you will learn to work with measurements, convert between different units of measure, and determine how precise your measurements should be. You will also learn how to recognize and use formulas.

# Measurement on the Job

## Build on What You Know

Think about the ways that you use measurement in your life. Maybe you checked the amount of gas in your gas tank and figured out the distance between your home and somewhere you needed to be. Then you calculated how long it would take you to get there. Each of those actions involved measurement in some way. When you make a schedule, determine the cost to ship a package, or figure out the dimensions of a space or an object, you are also using measurement in various ways.

When you measure something, you may need to decide which unit to use. Different types of measurements use different units, and the unit you will use depends on the type of measurement you need to take. There are also different tools that you can use to help you take measurements. Choosing the appropriate unit and tool is very important so that you can be sure that your measurement will be accurate.

The U.S. uses a measurement system called the **customary measurement system**. Within this system, there are standard units that are used to measure length (or distance), weight, and capacity.

### In Real Life   What's the Measure?

Alejandro is working as a welder. His supervisor gives him a set of blueprints for an upcoming job and asks him to verify the measurements and make any necessary adjustments. After he has checked the blueprints, his supervisor asks him to start cutting the pieces of sheet metal that they will need to complete the job.

 **Discuss the following questions with a classmate. Share your ideas with the class.**

1. Will Alejandro be measuring length, weight, or capacity when he double-checks the measurements in the blueprints?

2. What measuring tools might Alejandro use to verify the blueprints and to begin cutting the sheet metal?

3. What units of measure will Alejandro use when completing these tasks? Might he use more than one unit of measure? Explain.

# Solving Measurement Problems

The lessons in Chapter 1 taught you about the steps to follow when solving a problem.

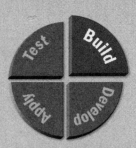

- Understand the problem by reading the problem carefully.
- Develop a plan by identifying the key words, operations, and strategies that are necessary to solve the problem.
- Work the problem by following your plan.
- Check to make sure your answer is reasonable.

These steps remain the same when the problem involves measurement. Measurement problems may have key words that indicate the type of measurement or the units involved. There may also be other clues to help you determine which units or type of measurement you should use, if this information is not given to you.

 **Read the following scenarios. Decide whether the scenario requires you to use or find some type of measurement. Share your ideas with the class.**

> **Workplace Tip**
>
> Remember, a problem may not involve measurement simply because it contains units of measurement. Read the problem carefully to see if the units are relevant to the solution.

4. You meet with your supervisor to go over the tasks that have to be completed today. You take notes on an 8.5- by 14-inch legal pad.

5. Your supervisor asks you to determine how many crates can be loaded onto a truck so that the truck is not over its weight limit.

6. You are checking an expense report for one of the traveling salespeople in your office. The salesperson is reimbursed for the mileage he drove.

7. You work at a hardware store. You are asked to determine how many tape measures you need to purchase to restock the store's inventory.

# Types of Measurement

There are three basic types of measurement you will learn about in this lesson: length, weight, and capacity.

- **Length** is the measure of the distance between two points. Often when you are measuring the length of an object, you measure from one end to the other. To measure length, you use units such as inches, feet, yards, and miles.
- **Weight** is the measure of how heavy something is. Measuring weight uses units such as ounces, pounds, and tons.
- **Capacity** is a measure of how much an object can hold. It is measured using units such as fluid ounces, cups, pints, quarts, and gallons.

 **Think about each type of measurement discussed above. Name at least one way that you have used or seen each type of measurement used.**

# Develop Your Skills

It is important to be able to recognize and use the appropriate tools and units when working with measurement. For example, if you need to find the dimensions of a room in order to figure out how much carpet to install, you would likely use a tape measure instead of a ruler. Both are tools that measure length, but the tape measure allows you to measure distances longer than a foot. If you used a ruler, you would have to measure each dimension foot by foot, marking an endpoint and then starting again until you found the total length. Not only would this be fairly boring and time-consuming, but you would likely end up with a less accurate measurement.

## Choose the Appropriate Tool

There are many different types of measuring tools. You are probably familiar with rulers, which are used to measure length. Other tools that measure length include yardsticks, tape measures, and odometers (used in vehicles to measure distance traveled). Weight is measured using scales and balances.

Capacity can be measured using a variety of items. One of the most common ways to measure capacity is to use measuring cups. The name of this tool is a little misleading, since the capacity of a measuring cup is not necessarily 1 cup. A measuring cup has labels or markings that indicate the measure or measures that can be taken. For example, a common measuring cup that many people use for cooking and baking has a capacity of 2 cups, with markings to show measures such as $\frac{1}{4}$ cup, $\frac{1}{2}$ cup, $1\frac{1}{3}$ cups, and so on.

 **Read each scenario and determine the appropriate tool to use.**

1. You are working for a company as a mail clerk. One of your responsibilities is to process all of the packages that need to go out each night. You need to weigh each package and use the postage meter to purchase the appropriate amount of postage.

2. You are preparing food to be served in the company cafeteria. Each day, you make a number of prepackaged meals so that people may take their food to go. Today you are preparing a chef's salad. Each salad should contain $1\frac{1}{2}$ cups of lettuce.

3. The construction company you are working for has been hired to remodel a bathroom. Your job is to measure and prepare the surfaces in the bathroom that are going to be tiled.

# Working with Measurement

When you work with measurement, you will often work with amounts that include parts of a whole. You can express a measure that includes a part as a fraction or a decimal. Many business supplies and tools have measures that include fractions or decimals. For example, a standard size of copy paper measures 8.5 inches wide and 11 inches long. Building supplies come in many different sizes that include fractional lengths, widths, and heights.

It is important to understand how precise you need to be when taking measurements. If you are figuring out how much paint you will need to paint a room, you probably only need to find a rough measure of the square footage of each wall. However, if you are giving a patient medication, it is very important to give exactly the prescribed amount.

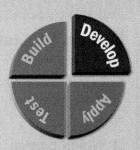

### Example:

Morgen's company is hired to install a brick patio. Her boss asks her to go to the customer's home and take measurements of the space where the patio will be installed. The measurements will be used to determine an estimate for the customer and to determine some of the materials that need to be purchased for the job. What measurements will Morgen take? Which tool or tools should she use? How accurate should Morgen be? *Morgen will be measuring the length and width to determine the area of the patio. She should use a tape measure. She will need to be quite accurate and so should probably measure in feet and inches.*

### Example:

As a truck driver who hauls gravel, dirt, and asphalt, you are paid for the weight of each load you deliver and the distance you must drive from the quarry to the delivery site. What measurements need to be taken when you arrive at the job site in order for you to be paid accurately? What tools should be used? How accurate do the measurements need to be? *You should record the odometer reading when you leave the quarry and when you arrive at the job site in order to figure out the distance you drove. You should also use a scale to measure the weight of your load. Since you are hauling large amounts of material, your load will probably be measured in tons or pounds.*

> ## Workplace Tip
> Sometimes you will see or use more than one unit of measure when taking measurements or solving measurement problems. In the example, it may make sense to use both feet and inches when measuring these dimensions, since it is unlikely that the dimensions will measure an exact number of feet.

## GOT IT? To solve problems in the workplace involving measurement, you must:

- Know what type of measurement you need to find.

- Determine the measurement tool that is best suited for the situation.

- Identify the unit(s) of measurement you are working with and how precise your measurements need to be.

**Answer Key**

**1.** scale

**2.** measuring cup

**3.** ruler or tape measure

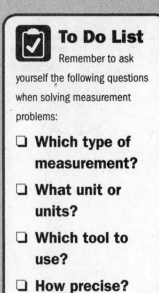
# Apply Your Knowledge

Solving problems that involve measurement requires that you understand basic units of measurement and the various tools that can be used to find each type of measurement.

**As you read the following scenarios, think about what the problem is asking you to find. Answer the key questions and select the correct answer.**

1. You are preparing to set up a new clothing display at a department store. Your supervisor tells you the measurements for the display should be 4 × 4. However, she forgot to say which unit of measurement to use. Which unit of measurement did she most likely intend for you to use?

   • What type of measurement is being used in the scenario?

   • When making this type of measurement, what are the different units that you might use?

   A. inches

   B. pounds

   C. feet

   D. miles

2. As a line chef in a restaurant, you need to measure ingredients when making sauces and other components of the dishes you create. Which measurement tool would you use to measure your ingredients?

   • What type of measurement is being used in the scenario?

   • What are the different units used in this type of measurement?

   A. thermometer

   B. tape measure

   C. ruler

   D. measuring cup

3. You are a nurse's aide in a hospital. You need to replenish the floor's supplies of intravenous fluid. Which unit of measure is the fluid most likely measured in?

   A. gallons

   B. pints

   C. pounds

   D. inches

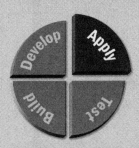

4. The sign below shows the lengths of some fence posts sold in a lumber store. Some customers have found the measurements to be confusing, so you are going to change the sign. Which unit would make more sense to use?

| Length of Post | Cost |
|---|---|
| 48 in. | $5 |
| 60 in. | $7 |
| 84 in. | $10 |
| 96 in. | $12 |

A. feet

B. tons

C. miles

D. pounds

## In Real Life  Put Your Skills to Work!

You are a construction worker who does a variety of jobs on the work site. You do general work in carpentry, plumbing, masonry, and concrete. Each job requires a specific skill and the ability to use measurement in different ways. In order to do your job effectively, you must be capable of finding a variety of measurements. You must also know which measurement tools you will need to have at the job site.

 **Think about the problem you are facing and put your skills to work! What is an example of each type of measurement that would be used? Which tools would you need to have available to take the necessary measurement in each situation?**

**Workplace Tip**

When making your decision, did you:

- Think about the correct type of measurement in each case?
- Use the units of measurement that make sense in each case?
- Select appropriate tools for measurement?

## Think About It!

**What types of measurement do you normally use in your workplace?**

**How do you decide on the best unit of measurement to use?**

**What types of tools do you have available for measurement in your job?**

In most jobs, there will be times when you need to take measurements or solve measurement problems. You may need to determine what type of measurement you should take, what the appropriate unit or units are, and which tool which will give you the most accurate measurement.

**Answer Key**

1. C
2. D
3. B
4. A

# Test Your WRC Skills

**Read the following scenarios. Select which answer you think is the correct response.**

1. You are a carpenter installing a wood deck for a customer. Before you start to build the deck, you must measure the area in order to know how much wood you will need. Which unit of measure would you most likely use for the deck's dimensions?

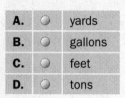

| A. | ○ | yards |
|----|----|-------|
| B. | ○ | gallons |
| C. | ○ | feet |
| D. | ○ | tons |

2. As a butcher, you sell meat, poultry, and fish by weight. A customer orders $1\frac{1}{2}$ pounds of chicken. Which tool would you use to measure out the amount of chicken the customer has ordered?

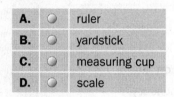

| A. | ○ | ruler |
|----|----|-------|
| B. | ○ | yardstick |
| C. | ○ | measuring cup |
| D. | ○ | scale |

3. You are working in a bakery. A customer has ordered a wedding cake. The recipe calls for ingredients such as flour and sugar. What unit of measurement would you most likely use for these ingredients?

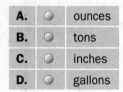

| A. | ○ | ounces |
|----|----|-------|
| B. | ○ | tons |
| C. | ○ | inches |
| D. | ○ | gallons |

4. Your supervisor gives you measurements to make a custom picture frame for a customer. The order sheet gives the frame measurements of 13.5 by 20.75. Your supervisor forgot to indicate what units to use. Which units did your supervisor most likely intend to write down with the measurements?

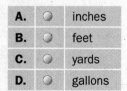

| A. | ○ | inches |
|----|----|-------|
| B. | ○ | feet |
| C. | ○ | yards |
| D. | ○ | gallons |

5. You are a truck driver. Your pay is partly determined by the distance that you drive. Which unit of measurement is most likely used when measuring the distance that you drive?

| A. | ○ | feet |
|----|---|------|
| B. | ○ | yards |
| C. | ○ | tons |
| D. | ○ | miles |

6. You are working as a roofer. You have gone to the home-supply store to get a supply of roofing nails. Which of the following measurements would be a reasonable measure of the roofing nails that you need to purchase?

| A. | ○ | $\frac{3}{4}$ ft |
|----|---|------|
| B. | ○ | $\frac{3}{4}$ yd |
| C. | ○ | $\frac{3}{4}$ lb |
| D. | ○ | $\frac{3}{4}$ in. |

7. Which of the following measurements is an appropriate weight for a single brick patio paver?

| A. | ○ | 5 oz |
|----|---|------|
| B. | ○ | 5 lb |
| C. | ○ | 5 t |
| D. | ○ | 5 gal |

8. You are hired to install hardwood flooring for a customer. The first thing you need to do is determine how much flooring you need. Which tool would you use to find the dimensions of the room?

| A. | ○ | tape measure |
|----|---|------|
| B. | ○ | protractor |
| C. | ○ | measuring cup |
| D. | ○ | compass |

**Check your answers on page 153.**

# Conversions

## Build on What You Know

Think about a situation at home or at work where you had to measure something. How did you select the appropriate units? Did you have the tools necessary to complete the measurements? Perhaps you had to **convert**, or change the measurement from one unit to another.

As you have seen in previous lessons, working with measurement is a regular part of most jobs. It is important for you to know the appropriate units of measurement and which tools to use to find a measurement. In this lesson, you will learn how to convert between different units. You will need to use the problem-solving skills you have developed to solve problems that require unit conversion.

**Essential Tasks**

**Convert common units of measure** from one system to another using informal methods

**Determine whether to add, subtract, multiply, or divide** to solve a problem

**Workplace Tip**

It is important to pay close attention to the units given in the problem. It may be helpful to circle the given units. When solving measurement problems, you should also double-check your answer to make sure you have given it in the correct units.

### In Real Life   How Long Is It?

You are working in a home-improvement store. Today, your job is to help customers in the rug department. A customer wants to purchase a rug for his hallway. The length of the hallway is 60 inches. Your store sells throw rugs, but they are priced and sold by the foot. The customer would like to know how much he will pay for a rug that will run the whole length of his hallway.

 **With a classmate, discuss the following questions. Share your ideas with the class.**

1. What are the important facts in this problem?

2. What information do you need that is not stated in the problem?

3. Will the number of feet be more or less than the number of inches stated in the problem?

## Measurement Units and Tools

Units are an essential part of measurement. Imagine trying to make a recipe without knowing the units for each ingredient or trying to build something without knowing the dimensions of the space you have to build it in.

You learned in the last lesson about three types of measurement that are often used in the workplace. Each type of measurement has certain units associated with it. These are shown in the table on the following page.

**Teacher Reminder**

Review the teacher lesson at www.mysteckvaughn.com/WORK

| Type | Common Units |
|------|--------------|
| Length | inches, feet, yards, miles |
| Capacity | cups, pints, quarts, gallons |
| Weight | ounces, pounds, tons |

As you learned in Lesson 7, there are different tools that you can use to make each type of measurement. Choosing the appropriate tool is an important part of taking measurements. For example, if you need to measure the dimensions of a room, you will need a tape measure rather than a scale or a measuring cup. Sometimes the tool required will be determined by the size of the units involved in the problem. Again, if you need to find the dimensions of a room, it would be much simpler and quicker to use a tape measure than a ruler.

 **Read the following scenarios. Decide which type of measurement and which unit should be used. Then decide on the appropriate tool. Share your ideas with the class.**

4. You are loading a two-wheeler for a co-worker to wheel into a store. You need to be careful not to stack too many boxes so that the load is not too heavy for her.

5. A customer brings a poster in to the frame shop where you work to get it framed. You need to measure the poster to determine the size of the frame.

6. You need to mix enough punch to serve all of the people attending a party. Each punch bowl can hold two gallons of punch, and there are five different ingredients you need to mix to make each batch.

## Converting Among Units

A measurement may be given in a number of different ways. For example, 5 cups can also be expressed as 2.5 pints or 1.25 quarts. These different ways of expressing a measurement are **equivalent**, or equal in value.

Knowing how to convert from one unit of measurement to another is an important and useful measurement skill. You can only convert measurements of the same type from one unit to another. For example, you can convert inches to feet, yards, or miles, but you can't convert them to cups or pounds.

 **Think about a time when you needed to convert from one unit to another. How did you know you needed to convert? How did you carry out the conversion? Share your ideas with the class.**

# Develop Your Skills

When solving measurement problems, you may be given a measurement in one unit but asked to give the answer in another unit. In order to convert, you must know the equivalent measure. You must also determine whether you are converting from larger to smaller units or from smaller to larger units. This will help you figure out which operation to use to convert.

## Equivalent Measures

The tables below show you some equivalent measures.

| Length | Weight | Capacity |
|---|---|---|
| 12 inches = 1 foot | 16 ounces = 1 pound | 8 fluid ounces = 1 cup |
| 3 feet = 1 yard | 2,000 pounds = 1 ton | 2 cups = 1 pint |
| 1,760 yards = 1 mile | | 2 pints = 1 quart |
| | | 4 quarts = 1 gallon |

## Converting from Larger to Smaller Units

When converting from larger to smaller units, you **multiply** by the equivalent unit value. For example, a conversion from pounds to ounces is a conversion from larger units to smaller units. Since there are 16 ounces in a pound, you multiply the number of pounds by 16. Write the equivalent units as a fraction. The smaller unit should be in the numerator and the larger unit is in the denominator. Then when you multiply, the units will cancel, as shown below, leaving you with the units to which you are converting.

$$2\,\text{lb} \times \left( \frac{16\ \text{oz}}{1\ \text{lb}} \right) = 32\ \text{oz}$$

**Example:**

A customer has asked you for the price on 25 yards of baseboard he needs for a remodeling project. The store where you work prices baseboard at $7.00 per foot. How would you solve this problem? *The information in the problem is given in yards and feet. You need to find the number of feet in 25 yards. Since you are going from a larger unit to a smaller unit, you need to multiply. Using equivalent measures, you know there are 3 feet in 1 yard. 25 yards $\times \frac{3\ feet}{1\ yard}$ = 75 feet. Finally, multiply the number of feet (75) by $7.00 to find the total price of $525.00.*

## Converting from Smaller to Larger Units

When you are converting from smaller units to larger units, you **divide** by the equivalent unit value. For example, a conversion from ounces to pounds is a conversion from smaller units to larger units. Since there are 16 ounces in a pound, you divide the number of ounces by 16.

Write the equivalent units as a fraction. The smaller unit should be in the numerator and the larger unit is in the denominator. When you divide by a fraction, you have to multiply by its reciprocal. Do the calculations. The units will cancel, leaving the unit to which you are converting.

$$32 \text{ oz} \div \left(\frac{16 \text{ oz}}{1 \text{ lb}}\right) = 32 \text{ oz} \times \left(\frac{1 \text{ lb}}{16 \text{ oz}}\right) = 2 \text{ lb}$$

**Example:**

Your work truck is rated to carry up to 10,000 pounds. How many tons can your truck carry? *The information is given in pounds. You need to find the number of tons in 10,000 pounds. Since you are going from a smaller unit to a larger unit, you need to divide. Using equivalent measures, you know there are 2,000 pounds in 1 ton.*

$10,000 \text{ pounds} \div \frac{2,000 \text{ pounds}}{1 \text{ ton}} = 10,000 \text{ pounds} \times \frac{1 \text{ ton}}{2,000 \text{ pounds}} = 5 \text{ tons}.$

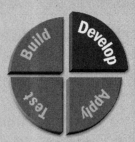

> **Workplace Tip**
>
> When converting units, always ask yourself if you should end up with a larger number or a smaller number. Remember that there should always be more of the smaller units to be equivalent. This will help you to determine if your answer is reasonable.

## In Real Life — What Is the Correct Amount?

The company you work for has been contracted to lay down a blacktop bike path that measures 0.75 miles. The supplier of blacktop needs to know the number of yards of blacktop you will be laying. You will also be painting a line down the middle of the path. The paint supplier needs to know the length in feet of the line you will be painting.

 **With a classmate, discuss the following questions. Share your ideas with the class.**

1. In what unit is the measure in this problem given? What units are required to answer each question?

2. Do you need to convert from smaller to larger units or larger to smaller units?

3. What operation(s) should be used for each conversion?

4. What measure will you give the blacktop supplier?

5. What measure will you give the paint supplier?

---

**GOT IT?** In order to solve problems involving unit conversions, you must:

- Identify the units given and the units required in the answer.
- Multiply if you are converting from larger units to smaller units.
- Divide if you are converting from smaller units to larger units.

**Answer Key**

1. miles; yards for blacktop and feet for paint
2. larger to smaller for both: miles to yards and miles or yards to feet
3. multiplication
4. 1,320 yd
5. 3,960 ft

## To Do List

Remember to use these steps when applying your knowledge:

- ❏ **Determine what units are given and what units are needed for the solution.**

- ❏ **Figure out if the unit conversion is from smaller to larger or larger to smaller.**

- ❏ **Use the correct operation for the conversion.**

# Apply Your Knowledge

In order to solve real-world problems involving unit conversion, you must know the equivalent measures to use for the conversion. You must also decide if you will multiply or divide to complete the conversion.

**As you read the following scenarios, think about what the problem is asking you to do. Answer the key questions and select the correct answer.**

1. You are using a forklift to load pallets of food onto a truck. You know that each pallet weighs 500 pounds. How many pallets can you load onto the truck if the maximum weight load for the truck is 5 tons?

   - What units are given and what units are required for the answer?
   - Is the conversion from larger to smaller units or smaller to larger units?
   - What operation is used for the conversion?

   A.  20

   B.  100

   C.  400

   D. 10,000

2. As a clerk in a fish store, you are responsible for filling the new fish aquariums. The one you must fill today can hold 10 gallons. You have a quart container you are using to carry water from the water source to the aquarium. How many trips will you need to make to fill the aquarium?

   A. 2.5

   B. 5

   C. 20

   D. 40

3. You get paid by the mile when making deliveries. The first delivery on your route is only 2,640 feet from your warehouse. How many miles will you get paid for on your first stop?

   A. 0.5 mi

   B. 2 mi

   C. 2.5 mi

   D. 5 mi

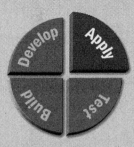

## In Real Life  Put Your Skills to Work!

In your job as a line cook, you deal with measurement every day. When you are prepping before a meal service, you must measure out large amounts of ingredients to make some of the components of the various dishes. You must also prepare large amounts of each ingredient that you will use to make each meal to order during service.

When you are working the line at a meal service, you must weigh and portion out pieces of meat and fish when preparing meals. You must also measure out ingredients when preparing the food that goes with each dish, as well as making sauces and other components when the orders come in.

 **Think about the problem you are facing and put your skills to work! Which measurement tools would you use during prep and meal service? When might you need to convert from smaller units to larger units? When might you need to convert from larger units to smaller units?**

## Think About It!

**What are some situations at work or in everyday life where you had to convert units of measure in order to accomplish a task or solve a problem?**

**What strategies do you use to help you remember how to convert between units?**

When solving problems involving measurement, remember the problem-solving skills that you have learned. Read the problem carefully and restate the question in your own words to determine if the units must be converted. If the units do need to be converted, you must decide if you are converting from larger to smaller, in which case you would multiply, or smaller to larger, in which case you would divide. When converting, be sure that you are using the correct equivalent units. Remember that each type of measurement deals with different units. Once you have completed the unit conversion, you should look at your answer to see if it is reasonable.

# Test Your WRC Skills

**Read each problem scenario. Select which answer you think is the correct response.**

1. The landscape company you work for is laying new sod on a football field. The football field is 120 yards long, including both end zones. The sod you are laying comes in 6-foot lengths. How many pieces of sod will it take to cover the length of the field?

   | A. | ○ | 20 pieces |
   |----|---|-----------|
   | B. | ○ | 60 pieces |
   | C. | ○ | 120 pieces |
   | D. | ○ | 360 pieces |

2. A recipe you are preparing for a wedding reception calls for a pint of buttermilk. You need to double the recipe to make enough servings for all the guests. The measuring cup that you are using has a 1-cup capacity. How many cups of buttermilk should you add to the recipe?

   | A. | ○ | 1 c |
   |----|---|-----|
   | B. | ○ | 2 c |
   | C. | ○ | 4 c |
   | D. | ○ | 8 c |

3. You are working as a shipping clerk. A customer brings in a large envelope that weighs 20 ounces. You need to convert this measurement to pounds to determine how much to charge the customer. What is this measure in pounds?

   | A. | ○ | 1 lb |
   |----|---|------|
   | B. | ○ | 1.25 lb |
   | C. | ○ | 4 oz |
   | D. | ○ | 320 oz |

4. A customer brings in a print that she would like framed. The dimensions of the print are 16 inches by 20 inches. Your framing supplier prices its supplies by the foot. What are the dimensions of the print in feet?

   | A. | ○ | 4 ft by 5 ft |
   |----|---|--------------|
   | B. | ○ | $1\frac{1}{3}$ ft by $1\frac{2}{3}$ ft |
   | C. | ○ | $3\frac{1}{3}$ ft by 4 ft |
   | D. | ○ | 192 ft by 240 ft |

5. You need to use 0.25 cup of olive oil for each batch of vinaigrette dressing that you prepare in your job as a prep cook. The chef asks you to increase the amount of dressing you prepare each day so that you are making 10 batches of dressing. If your supplier sells olive oil by the gallon, how many gallons of oil will you need to tell the chef to order for one week?

| A. | ○ | 280 gal |
| B. | ○ | 0.1 gal |
| C. | ○ | 1 gal |
| D. | ○ | 2 gal |

6. You sell coffee beans in bulk by the pound. You must weigh each bag of beans individually to find the weight. A customer brings a bag of beans to the counter that weighs 36 ounces. How many pounds of beans does the customer want to purchase?

| A. | ○ | 1 lb |
| B. | ○ | 2.25 lb |
| C. | ○ | 2.5 lb |
| D. | ○ | 576 lb |

7. As a nurse's aide, you read the doctor's instructions to the patient. During recovery, the doctor wants to make sure the patient stays hydrated. She orders the patient to consume 16 cups of water each day. The patient has a quart pitcher he uses to measure his consumption each day. How many quarts of water does he need to drink?

| A. | ○ | 1 qt |
| B. | ○ | 2 qt |
| C. | ○ | 4 qt |
| D. | ○ | 64 qt |

Check your answers on page 154.

# Formulas

**Essential Tasks**

**Recognize and use simple formulas** (such as $d = rt$)

**Determine whether to add, subtract, multiply, or divide** to solve a problem

## Build on What You Know

Have you ever needed to figure out how much paint you needed to cover the walls in a room or how much carpet would cover a floor? Solving these types of measurement problems requires you to do more than take a measurement using the appropriate tool. Maybe you knew the distance that you needed to travel and the route you needed to take and wanted to figure out how long it would take you to get there. When you need to solve these types of problems, there are formulas that can help you.

A mathematical **formula** is an equation that represents a relationship between values. You have likely learned and used some formulas before. Understanding formulas and being able to use them will help you perform your job more efficiently.

### In Real Life · Using a Formula

Trevor is installing a fence around a rectangular-shaped dog kennel for a customer. He measures the sides of the space around the kennel where the fence is to be installed. He finds the length of one side is 10 feet and the length of the other side is 15 feet.

 **Discuss the following questions with a classmate. Share your ideas with the class.**

1. What is Trevor trying to determine by taking the measurements?

2. Is there a formula that can be used to solve this problem? What is the formula?

3. How does this help Trevor plan for the project?

## Problem Solving with Measurement

In Lessons 7 and 8, you learned how to solve problems involving measurement. Continue to follow the steps that you have learned for all problem-solving, including reading the problem carefully, making a plan, choosing a strategy, solving, and checking your answer for reasonableness. Also be sure to remember the following points that may be involved when solving measurement problems:

**Teacher Reminder**

Review the teacher lesson at www.mysteckvaughn.com/WORK

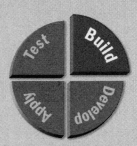

- Identify the units given and the units that are required in the answer.
- Convert the units of measurement, if necessary, by multiplying or dividing using equivalent measures.

## Using Formulas to Solve Measurement Problems

As you read above, a formula expresses a relationship between quantities or measurements. It is important that you understand what each part of a formula represents so that you can identify which formula to use in a particular situation and which values to substitute into the formula to solve correctly. In this lesson, you will learn several formulas that can help you when solving measurement problems.

The first formula will help when you need to find perimeter. **Perimeter** is the distance around a figure. If you know the measures of each of the sides of a figure, you can add them together to find the perimeter. You may often need to find the perimeter of a rectangular space. Since opposite sides of a rectangle are equal, you can use the formula $P = 2l + 2w$ to find perimeter.

The distance around a circular figure is called its **circumference**. To find circumference, use the formula $C = \pi d$. The symbol $\pi$ stands for a mathematical value called *pi*. *Pi* is a **constant**, which means that it doesn't change—it has the same value every time you use it. When solving formulas with $\pi$, use the value 3.14 or $\frac{22}{7}$. The $d$ stands for the diameter of the circle.

The measure of the size of a surface is called its **area**. Area is measured in square units such as square feet. To find the area of a rectangular space, use the formula $A = l \times w$, where $l$ equals length and $w$ equals width.

**Volume** is the amount of space inside a three-dimensional figure such as a box. The formula to use when finding volume is $V = l \times w \times h$, where $l$ equals length, $w$ equals width, and $h$ equals height.

The distance formula represents the relationship between distance traveled, rate of speed, and time. This relationship is shown in the formula $D = r \times t$ or $D = rt$.

 **Discuss the following questions with a classmate. Share your ideas with the class.**

4. For which types of problems would you use a formula to help you solve?

5. Describe a scenario in which you would use a formula to solve a measurement problem.

6. How can formulas help you solve measurement problems?

# Develop Your Skills

To identify when a formula applies to a particular problem, you must read the entire problem carefully and understand what the problem is asking. Then incorporate the formula that fits into your problem-solving strategy.

## Identify the Formula

When solving problems, you must be able to identify which formula to use. Think about what you have learned about measurement and each formula to help you figure out which one to use. If the problem doesn't tell you which formula to use, ask yourself questions such as:

- What measurements are given to me?
- What shape or shapes are involved in the problem?
- How many dimensions are given to me in the problem? Do I need to use every one or are some of them extra, irrelevant information?

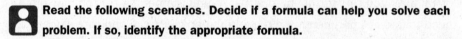 **Read the following scenarios. Decide if a formula can help you solve each problem. If so, identify the appropriate formula.**

1. You are building a deck that measures 20 feet by 30 feet and you need to know how many decking boards you will need.

2. Your supervisor asks you to make a delivery 40 miles away. You need to be there in 50 minutes. At what rate of speed do you need to travel in order to arrive in time?

3. You are working in a package-supply store. A customer asks you the dimensions of a certain box you sell. He wants to know how much will fit inside the box.

4. You need to figure out how much icing to make so that you can make a decorative border around the top and bottom of a cake.

5. You are asked to put a chicken wire fence around a rectangular garden. How much fence do you need?

## Use Formulas to Solve Problems

Once you have identified the correct formula to use, you need to be able to substitute the information you are given into the formula to answer the question. You may find it helpful to write out the formula. Then underline or circle the information in the problem that gives you the values you will need to substitute into the formula. This can help you keep track of what you know and what you need to find.

Sometimes you are asked to find the value of an unknown measure such as the time that it will take you to get somewhere. Simply substitute the values that you do know into the formula and solve.

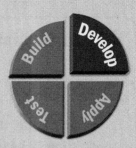

**Example:**

Drake is planting new grass in a rectangular area for a customer. His charges are calculated per square foot. The dimensions of the space are 30 feet by 45 feet. What does he need to do first in order to figure out how much to charge the customer? *He needs to find the area of the space using the formula $A = l \times w$. $A = 30 \times 45 = 1{,}350$ square feet*

**Example:**

Tomas needs to find the volume of a crate that he is shipping. The crate is 36 inches long by 24 inches wide by 18 inches tall. What is the volume of the crate? *$V = l \times w \times h = 36 \times 24 \times 18 = 15{,}552$ cubic inches*

**Example:**

You need to visit a patient at her home. She lives 25 miles from the hospital. The average speed along the route you will take is 40 miles per hour. How long will it take you to get there? *You know the distance you are traveling and the average rate of speed. Use the distance formula $D = r \times t$ and substitute the values you know: $25 = 40 \times t$. Then solve and convert the answer, 0.625 hours, into minutes by multiplying by 60. It will take you 37.5 minutes to get to the patient's house.*

**In Real Life** **Landscaping Duty**

You work for a landscaping company that determines what to charge using the square footage for each job. You are working on a flower bed that measures 12 yards by 35 yards. If your company charges $0.10 per square foot, how much will the customer be charged?

 **Imagine that you need to calculate the required information. Ask yourself the following questions.**

6. What is the first thing you need to find? What formula will you use?

7. Do you need to convert units to solve?

8. How much will you charge the customer?

| **GOT IT?** | **To use formulas to help you solve measurement problems, you should:** |
|---|---|

- Understand what the question is asking you to find.
- Determine which units you are given and which units the answer requires.
- Figure out what formula you should use.
- Check to be sure your answer is reasonable.

**Workplace Tip**

Remember that when you are using a formula to solve, you substitute values into the formula. If you know two of the values that you will substitute into the formula, you can find the third value that is unknown, no matter what part of the formula it is.

**Answer Key**

1. area; $A = l \times w$

2. distance; $D = r \times t$

3. volume; $V = l \times w \times h$

4. circumference; $C = \pi d$

5. perimeter; $P = 2l \times 2w$

6. the area of the flower bed; $A = l \times w$

7. Yes, you need to convert yards to feet.

8. $378.00

# Apply Your Knowledge

Now that you understand how and when to use different formulas in the workplace, apply the formulas you have learned to solve different real-world problems.

**Read each of the following scenarios. Then select the correct response for each question.**

1. Chang installs carpet for a flooring company. He receives an order from a customer who wants carpet put in his living room. If the room measures 14 feet by 20 feet, how much carpeting will Chang need to complete the job?

   A. 34 sq. ft

   B. 68 sq. ft

   C. 280 sq. ft

   D. 596 sq. ft

2. Brian works as an outside sales representative. He spends 5 hours on the road every day and drives at an average speed of 45 miles per hour. What is the total distance he travels each day?

   A. 9 mi

   B. 50 mi

   C. 225 mi

   D. 450 mi

3. Chelsea works at a bakery. She needs to make several pumpkin pies for a special order. She knows the circumference of her pie plates is 25.12 inches, but her recipe for pie crust requires her to figure out the diameter of the pie plate. What is the diameter of one of Chelsea's pie plates?

   A. 8 in.

   B. 100.48 in.

   C. 200.96 in.

   D. 0.65 in.

## In Real Life — Put Your Skills to Work!

You just found a job as commercial truck driver. This job can be demanding because of the time you will spend on the road. It requires you to get a commercial driver's license and to sometimes work long days and nights. This job also requires you to schedule routes and times so that you can make all of your deliveries on a given day. In order to accomplish this, you need to know driving distances and the routes you will be taking. You may know the speed at which you can travel on these routes. You also need to be able to schedule the time needed for each pick-up and delivery time, as well as potential delays for traffic and construction.

 **Think about the problem you are facing and put your skills to work! What formula could you use to help you on the job? What information will help you be more organized and efficient at this job?**

### Workplace Tip

When reading the problem, did you think about:

- the units involved?
- the formula involved in finding the solution?
- how the measurements you will use fit into the formula?

## Think About It!

**What types of problems do you encounter at work or every day that might require you to use a formula to solve?**

**How do you know when it is appropriate or necessary to use a formula?**

There are many types of problems in the workplace that require you to use a formula to solve. If you have solved problems that deal with measurement, you probably have used a formula. To be able to use formulas accurately and effectively, it is important that you understand the scenario and the question being asked. As with other math problems, there are key words that can help you determine which formula to use. For example, if the question asks for the distance around an object, it is referring to perimeter. If the problem asks about square footage or yardage, it is referring to area. Common formulas used in the workplace include perimeter, circumference, area, volume, and distance. Knowing how to use these formulas confidently can help you do your job more efficiently and effectively.

**Answer Key**

1. C
2. C
3. A

# Test Your WRC Skills

**Solving mathematical problems may require you to use formulas. Read the following situations. Select which answer you think is the correct response.**

1. You are a commercial truck driver who has a delivery to make 200 miles away. You must be there in 4 hours. What speed must you average in order to get there on time?

| | | |
|---|---|---|
| **A.** | ○ | 4 mph |
| **B.** | ○ | 50 mph |
| **C.** | ○ | 60 mph |
| **D.** | ○ | 800 mph |

2. You are installing 3-inch-wide laminate flooring for a customer. The room in which you are installing the laminate is 12 feet wide by 20 feet long. How many square feet of flooring will you need for the floor?

| | | |
|---|---|---|
| **A.** | ○ | 32 sq. ft |
| **B.** | ○ | 36 sq. ft |
| **C.** | ○ | 60 sq. ft |
| **D.** | ○ | 240 sq. ft |

3. You work at a pet store that sells fish aquariums. A customer needs to know the amount of water an aquarium that is 12 inches long, 12 inches wide, and 12 inches deep can hold. Which of the following formulas would you use to answer the customer's question?

| | | |
|---|---|---|
| **A.** | ○ | $D = r \times t$ |
| **B.** | ○ | $A = l \times w$ |
| **C.** | ○ | $V = l \times w \times h$ |
| **D.** | ○ | $P = 2l + 2w$ |

4. Hans is building a fence for a customer who raises sheep. The area that the customer wants to be fenced measures 40 yards by 50 yards. The fence will be 1.5 yards tall. How much fencing will he need to complete the job?

| | | |
|---|---|---|
| **A.** | ○ | 90 yd |
| **B.** | ○ | 180 yd |
| **C.** | ○ | 2,000 yd |
| **D.** | ○ | 3,000 yd |

5.  Alfonzo works as a catering delivery driver. He has to make a delivery that is 30 miles away. If he averages 50 miles per hour, how long will it take him to arrive to his destination?

    | | | |
    |---|---|---|
    | **A.** | ○ | 36 min |
    | **B.** | ○ | 80 min |
    | **C.** | ○ | 1 hr 20 min |
    | **D.** | ○ | 20 hr |

6.  As a maintenance worker for a hardware store, you need to measure the distance around the inside of the store because you want to install new cove base (a rubber product that protects the base of a wall from damage). If the building is square, and one wall measures 45 feet, how much cove base (in feet) will you need to order?

    | | | |
    |---|---|---|
    | **A.** | ○ | 45 ft |
    | **B.** | ○ | 90 ft |
    | **C.** | ○ | 180 ft |
    | **D.** | ○ | 2,025 ft |

7.  A customer wants to purchase the largest sandbox that is carried at the home-improvement store where you are working. The table below shows the various sizes of the sandboxes that your store stocks. Which of these sandboxes has the largest area?

    | Sandbox Number | Sandbox Sizes |
    |---|---|
    | 1 | 12 ft × 12 ft |
    | 2 | 10 ft × 14 ft |
    | 3 | 8 ft × 16 ft |
    | 4 | 6 ft × 20 ft |

    | | | |
    |---|---|---|
    | **A.** | ○ | Sandbox 1 |
    | **B.** | ○ | Sandbox 2 |
    | **C.** | ○ | Sandbox 3 |
    | **D.** | ○ | Sandbox 4 |

Check your answers on page 155.

# Skills for the Workplace
## Precision—Rounding

Measurements in the workplace deal with more than just inches, pounds, and gallons. Businesses often use monetary measures to analyze how they are doing and whether they are making a profit. They may also use information about sales, profits or losses, expenses, and other items to determine whether they need to change the way they do business.

The lessons in this chapter discussed precision in measurement and the importance of recognizing the level of precision necessary when solving problems. In some cases, you need to be precise. In others, you can estimate.

Knowing how to estimate and round can also help you determine if your answers are reasonable. Remember, when rounding, look at the number to the right of the place to which you are rounding.

### Workplace Scenario

You are working as a data-entry clerk. Your boss has given you the financial statement shown below. You need to enter the information into a database. However, your boss said that you only need to enter each number rounded to the nearest billion.

| Annual Income Statement | |
|---|---|
| *all values in millions of dollars | |
| Total Revenue | 22,518.0 |
| Cost of Revenue, Total | 18,978.0 |
| Gross Profit | 5,413.0 |
| Operating Income | 1,291.0 |
| Income Before Tax | 1,611.0 |
| Income After Tax | 908.0 |

- How would you round the amount for total revenue to the nearest billion? *The amount is $22.5 billion. Since the number in the hundred millions place is 5, round up to $23 billion.*

- Are any of the amounts in the report less than $1 billion? How would you round that number? *Yes, the income after tax is $908 million. Round it up to $1 billion because the number in the hundred millions place is 9.*

- Of the other figures given in the report, which would you round up? Which would you round down? *Cost of Revenue, Total and Income Before Tax would get rounded up. Gross Profit and Operating Income would get rounded down.*

# Workplace Practice

You are working as a telemarketer for an Internet services company. Your supervisor has given you the following information on the profit margins for each product that you sell. Profit margin is a number that shows the ratio of profit to sales. It is often expressed as a percent.

| Domain Registration | 0.24% |
|---|---|
| Web Hosting Services | 9.8% |
| E-mail Accounts | 0.45% |
| Blog and Podcast Hosting | 6.5% |
| eCommerce Web site | 22.78% |
| Security Services | 11.47% |

- On which service does your company earn the greatest profit margin? *eCommerce Web site*

- What is the difference between the profit margin on Web Hosting Services and Blog and Podcast Hosting? *3.3%*

- Why do you think measures of profit margin are given to the tenths or hundredths decimal place? *Since profit margin is a measure of profitability for a company, it is important that it is measured as precisely as possible.*

## It's Your Turn!

1. Your boss gives you the income statement below and asks you to run some reports. She says that you can round each figure to the nearest billion.

| Annual Income Statement | |
|---|---|
| *all values in millions of dollars* | |
| **Total Revenue** | 42,905.0 |
| **Cost of Revenue, Total** | 26,812.0 |
| **Gross Profit** | 17,568.0 |
| **Operating Income** | 10,514.0 |
| **Income Before Tax** | 12,066.0 |
| **Income After Tax** | 8,461.0 |

   Which figure would round to $11 billion?

2. Why do you think it is more likely that you would use rounding and estimation when dealing with large numbers such as sales figures?

**Answer Key**

**1.** Operating Income

**2.** With large numbers such as sales figures, it is not necessary to know the exact figure down to the penny. Rounding the numbers will still give you a relatively accurate idea of what you are looking for and it makes the numbers easier to work with.

# Chapter 3 Assessment

**Read each problem and choose the best answer.**

1. You work on a road crew that paints lines on roads and highways. Your job is to measure the widths of lanes to ensure that the lines are painted the same width apart. You are measuring a turning lane that is 12 feet wide but the painting crew wants your measurement in yards. How many yards wide is the turning lane?

| A. | ○ | 3 yd |
|---|---|---|
| B. | ○ | 4 yd |
| C. | ○ | 6 yd |
| D. | ○ | 36 yd |

2. You are working in a donut shop. The recipe for the muffins you are baking says to add 120 ounces of flour. Which measuring tool would you use to meaure out the amount of flour the recipe indicates?

| A. | ○ | scale |
|---|---|---|
| B. | ○ | ruler |
| C. | ○ | tape measure |
| D. | ○ | tablespoon |

3. Jamie is hired by a carpet-cleaning service. The company charges $0.15 per square foot cleaned. If Jamie cleans a room that measures 12 feet by 14.5 feet, how much will Jamie charge the customer?

| A. | ○ | $2.61 |
|---|---|---|
| B. | ○ | $7.95 |
| C. | ○ | $26.10 |
| D. | ○ | $174.00 |

4. There is a summer sale on 32-ounce soft drinks at the fast-food restaurant where you are working. The cost of this soft drink is $0.99. If there are 8 ounces in one cup, how many cups are in the soft drink?

| A. | ○ | 4 c |
|---|---|---|
| B. | ○ | 24 c |
| C. | ○ | 31.68 c |
| D. | ○ | 256 c |

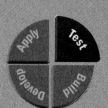

**5.** The table below shows the various sizes of aquariums you sell at the pet store. A customer wants to know which of the aquariums has the greatest volume. Which of the aquariums has the greatest volume in cubic inches?

| Aquarium Dimensions in Inches | |
| --- | --- |
| **1** | 12 × 8 × 8 |
| **2** | 12 × 12 × 12 |
| **3** | 12 × 10 × 14 |
| **4** | 20 × 10 × 10 |

| | | |
| --- | --- | --- |
| **A.** | ○ | Aquarium 1 |
| **B.** | ○ | Aquarium 2 |
| **C.** | ○ | Aquarium 3 |
| **D.** | ○ | Aquarium 4 |

**6.** A door frame that you are installing should measure 6 feet 8 inches tall. Your tape measure only shows units in inches. How many inches should the door frame be?

| | | |
| --- | --- | --- |
| **A.** | ○ | 14 in. |
| **B.** | ○ | 48 in. |
| **C.** | ○ | 72 in. |
| **D.** | ○ | 80 in. |

**7.** You are measuring the distance between two fence posts to determine the length of the fence panel that stretches between the fence posts. Which unit of measurement would you most likely use?

| | | |
| --- | --- | --- |
| **A.** | ○ | inches |
| **B.** | ○ | feet |
| **C.** | ○ | pounds |
| **D.** | ○ | gallons |

For more Chapter 3 assessment questions, please visit www.mysteckvaughn.com/WORK

Check your answers on page 156.

CHAPTER

# 4 Data

Data is often organized into graphic displays such as tables or charts. Being able to analyze data allows you to draw conclusions and make comparisons and predictions. In this chapter, you will analyze data by learning how to find the mean, median, mode, and range of a data set. You will read and interpret data in tables and charts and determine whether it is reliable. Finally, you will look at the variability of a data set and learn how to find the probability of an event.

# Compute Data

## Build on What You Know

In any job, you may be asked to work with sets of data. **Data** is organized, factual information. Data often takes the form of numbers, but data could also include names, dates, places, or events. At a hospital or clinic, you might work with data that describes a patient's health or medical history. At a store or warehouse, your job may involve data on inventory, suppliers, and customers. Don't forget that every business keeps data about money, such as salaries, costs, expenses, and taxes.

Regardless of the type or purpose of data, the same techniques and principles can help you analyze data and draw conclusions from it. Let's look at some examples.

### In Real Life   Five-pound Bags?

Terrell buys produce for a supermarket. The owner of an orchard offers to sell bags of apples to the store for $4.00 a bag. The owner states that each bag weighs approximately 5 pounds. To test this claim, Terrell chooses nine bags at random and weighs them on a scale. The data he obtains is shown in the table.

| Bags | 1 | 2 | 3 | 4 | 5 | 6 | 7 | 8 | 9 |
|---|---|---|---|---|---|---|---|---|---|
| Weight (lb) | 4.7 | 5.0 | 5.3 | 4.6 | 4.9 | 5.2 | 4.7 | 5.3 | 5.3 |

 **With a classmate, discuss the following questions. Share your ideas with the class.**

1. Does the data support the claim that each bag weighs approximately 5 pounds?

2. Should Terrell pay less for some bags and more for others, or should he agree to pay $4.00 for every bag?

## Analyzing Data

By examining a set of data, you often can draw a few simple conclusions. For example, after looking at the data set above, you can conclude that some of the bags of apples weigh slightly more than 5 pounds; others weigh slightly less. One weighs exactly 5 pounds.

**Teacher Reminder**
Review the teacher lesson at
www.mysteckvaughn.com/WORK

**114** Math

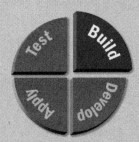

To answer certain questions about the data, however, you need to perform some calculations. For example, suppose you need to know what the greatest difference in weight between any two bags is. This value is called the range. The **range** of a set of data is the difference between its least and greatest values. Here the range is the difference between 5.3 pounds and 4.6 pounds, which is 0.7 pounds.

 **What is your guess for the range of ages among the people in the room? Discuss with the class.**

## Mean, Median, and Mode

When you analyze numerical data, it often helps to order the data from least to greatest. For the data on apples, the ordered set of weights looks like this:

| Weight (lb) | 4.6 | 4.7 | 4.7 | 4.9 | 5.0 | 5.2 | 5.3 | 5.3 | 5.3 |
|---|---|---|---|---|---|---|---|---|---|

The **median** of a set of data is the value exactly in the middle. For the data above, the median is 5.0 pounds. Four bags weigh more than 5.0 pounds, and four bags weigh less than 5.0 pounds. You can compare the median of a set of data to the median of a highway. Both are "in the middle."

The **mode** is the value that appears most often in a set of data. Here the mode is 5.3 pounds, which appears three times. Not all data sets have a mode. If every value in a data set is different, the data set has no mode. There may also be more than one mode in a data set. For example, if you replaced the bag of apples that weighed 4.6 pounds with one that weighed 4.7 pounds, then both 4.7 and 5.3 would be the mode of the data set, since both values would occur three times.

Finding the **mean**, which is sometimes called the average, requires some calculation. To find the mean, find the sum of the values, then divide by the number of values in the set. Here, the mean is found with this expression:

$(4.6 + 4.7 + 4.7 + 4.9 + 5.0 + 5.2 + 5.3 + 5.3 + 5.3) \div 9 = 5.0 \text{ lb}$

The mean may or may not be a value in the data set. The mean also may or may not be the same value as the median or mode.

 **With a classmate, discuss the following questions. Share your ideas with the class.**

3. Think of a data set in which the mean, median, and mode are the same value.

4. Of median, mode, and mean, which is easiest to calculate? Which is more difficult?

# Develop Your Skills

You can determine the range, mean, median, and mode for any set of numerical data. But rarely are all four values equally useful. Sometimes the mean is very important. If the daily sales at a store vary widely from Monday to Saturday, the store manager might want to know the mean sales for the six-day week. Other times the mode is most important. At a hospital, a patient's heart rate might increase greatly from time to time. The mode heart rate is a better indication of the patient's health.

## Calculations on Data

At any job, you might be called upon to use your best judgment to report either the range, mean, median, or mode of a data set, or some combination of these values. Think about this example.

**Example:**

Abby works at a day-care center. The ages of the children are listed from youngest to oldest in the table below.

| Child | 1 | 2 | 3 | 4 | 5 | 6 |
|---|---|---|---|---|---|---|
| Age (mo) | 12 | 14 | 17 | 19 | 21 | 25 |

For this data set, why is the mean or median useful for Abby to report, but not the mode? *The mean and median indicate the age of an average child at the day care. However, each child has a different age, so there is no mode.*

What is the mean age of the six children? *Add together the ages, then divide the sum by 6. The mean age is 18 months. Notice that in this example, the mean age is not a value in the data set.*

## Finding the Median

Look again at the data set of children's ages shown above. There are six values, so which is the median, or "middle" value? Both the third child (age 17 months) and fourth child (age 19 months) are equally close to the middle of the set of six children.

To calculate the median of a data set with an even number of data values, find the mean of the two values in the middle.

**Example:**

Abby wants to find the median of the children in the day care.
*The two values in the middle of the data set are 17 and 19.*
*17 + 19 = 36; 36 ÷ 2 = 18. The median age of the children in the day care is 18 months.*

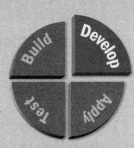

## In Real Life    Copier Repairs

You are working as receptionist at Birdsong Publishing. The company owns 30 copiers. The office manager asks you to prepare a report on the cost of repairing the copiers. The table presents data on the copiers for the first half of the year.

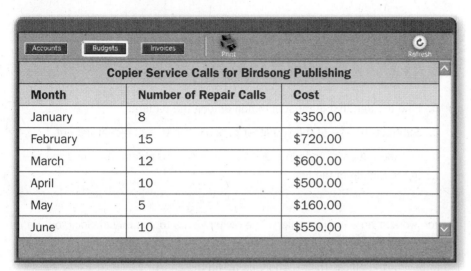

| Accounts | Budgets | Invoices |   | Print |   | Refresh |
|---|---|---|---|---|---|---|

### Copier Service Calls for Birdsong Publishing

| Month | Number of Repair Calls | Cost |
|---|---|---|
| January | 8 | $350.00 |
| February | 15 | $720.00 |
| March | 12 | $600.00 |
| April | 10 | $500.00 |
| May | 5 | $160.00 |
| June | 10 | $550.00 |

 **Answer the following questions.**

**1.** What is the range of the monthly number of repair calls?

**2.** What is the mean cost per month for repairing the copiers?

**3.** The office manager wants to know how many copier repair calls to expect for a typical month. What is a reasonable answer based on the data? Explain.

**4.** What additional information about the office copiers would help you prepare your report? Think of useful facts and recommendations you might include.

**Workplace Tip**

When you work with data in a table or spreadsheet, read the headings to the columns. Be sure to choose the correct column of data for the task you are completing.

## GOT IT?

Data is organized, factual information. To analyze a set of numerical data, you can find the following values:

- **Range:** the difference between the least and greatest values in the set
- **Mean:** the sum of the values in the set divided by the number of values
- **Median:** the "middle value" between the least and greatest values in the set
- **Mode:** the value or values that appear most often in the data set

**Answer Key**

**1.** 10

**2.** $480.00

**3.** The mean, median, and mode of the monthly number of repair calls all equal 10, so 10 is a reasonable answer.

**4.** You could ask for data on individual copiers, such as their amount of use, number of repairs, and the cost of their repairs. The data could help you recommend that a copier be replaced or eliminated.

 **To Do List**

Remember to follow these steps when applying your knowledge:

❑ **Identify what the question is asking in order to figure out which value or values may best help you answer the question.**

❑ **Arrange the values in a data set from least to greatest.**

❑ **Perform the necessary calculations to find the range, mean, median, or mode.**

# Apply Your Knowledge

The concepts of range, mean, median, and mode can apply to any set of numerical data. Use their definitions to solve these problems.

**Read each of the following scenarios and look at the data sets, if applicable. Select the correct response for each question.**

1. At a medical office, the office manager asks you to find the mode of the ages of the doctor's patients. How could you do this?

   A. Add together the ages of all the patients, then divide by the number of patients.

   B. Find the age that is most common among the patients.

   C. Subtract the age of the youngest patient from that of oldest patient.

   D. List the patients' ages in order from youngest to oldest, then find the age in the middle of the list.

2. You work at an antiques gallery. The owner wants to sell an old clock, but he is not sure what to charge for it. You ask 10 customers what they would expect to pay for the clock. Their responses are in the chart.

| Expected Price | $14 | $14 | $16 | $20 | $21 | $25 | $26 | $27 | $28 | $29 |
|---|---|---|---|---|---|---|---|---|---|---|

   What is the median price that the 10 customers would expect to pay?

   A. $14

   B. $20

   C. $22

   D. $23

3. In your job at a bank, you suspect a coin counter is working poorly. To test it, you carefully count out a set of coins that together are worth $15.00. Then you let the machine count them 12 times. The machine counts them correctly 10 times, but reports they are worth $15.25 and $14.95 the other two times.

   Which statement about the data set of machine coin counts is accurate?

   A. The mode of the data is $0.30

   B. The range of the data is $15.25.

   C. The mean of the data is $15.25.

   D. The median of the data is $15.00.

**Put Your Skills to Work!**

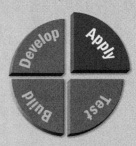

You just started a new job as the manager of a restaurant. The motto of the restaurant is: "The average price of our lunches is only $7.00!" However, some of the customers ask you if this claim is correct. To find out, you begin by reviewing the lunch menu, which is shown below.

| Lunch Menu | |
| --- | --- |
| *All items come with fries or steamed vegetables and a soft drink.* | |
| Hamburger | $8.00 |
| Mushroom burger | $8.50 |
| Ranch burger | $9.00 |
| Tuna salad | $7.50 |
| Steak sandwich | $11.00 |
| Egg salad | $5.50 |
| Chili (cup) | $4.50 |
| Chili (bowl) | $6.00 |

 **Is the restaurant's claim correct? If not, how could you change the prices on the menu so that the claim becomes correct?**

---

**Workplace Tip**

When answering the questions, did you think about:

- what the question was asking?
- which type of analysis you needed to make (range, mean, median, mode)?
- how you could change the data to achieve the desired result?

## Think About It!

Why is it helpful to list a set of numerical data from least to greatest values?

How are mean, median, and mode all alike? How are they different?

When is the mode useful for analyzing data? When is it not very useful?

As you have learned, math is all about problem solving. You now know how to find the range, mean, median, and mode of a set of data. Each of these four values is a tool that can help you analyze and interpret data for yourself, your co-workers, and others. If you served 100 customers during the workday, telling your boss the amount of money that each customer spent would take a long time and might not be very informative. Instead, reporting the mean amount that the customers spent is simpler and more useful. Being able to work with and analyze data can help you be a more effective employee.

**Answer Key**

**1.** B

**2.** D

**3.** D

# Test Your WRC Skills

**Read the following situations. Select which answer you think is the correct response.**

1. You report on baseball for the local newspaper. In the past 12 games, the home team scored the following number of runs: 8, 4, 0, 4, 7, 7, 8, 10, 1, 8, 2, and 10. What is the mode of the number of runs that the team scored?

   | | | |
   |---|---|---|
   | **A.** | ○ | 4 |
   | **B.** | ○ | 7 |
   | **C.** | ○ | 8 |
   | **D.** | ○ | 10 |

2. You work at a shoe store. The manager asks you to find the mean price of a certain type of shoe that your competitors sell. You call seven competitors and record the prices they quote for this shoe. How can you calculate the mean price?

   | | | |
   |---|---|---|
   | **A.** | ○ | Add the prices together and divide by the mode. |
   | **B.** | ○ | Add the prices together and divide by seven. |
   | **C.** | ○ | List the prices in order from least to greatest, and find the middle price. |
   | **D.** | ○ | Subtract the lowest price from the highest price. |

3. Your manager at the bakery asks you to review the prices of the bakery's donuts. You find that most types of donuts are sold for $0.50 each, but a few types are sold for higher prices. What further information do you need to find the range of the prices of donuts?

   | | | |
   |---|---|---|
   | **A.** | ○ | the price of the most expensive donut |
   | **B.** | ○ | the price of the customers' favorite donut |
   | **C.** | ○ | the number of donuts that the bakery sells each day |
   | **D.** | ○ | the number of donuts that sell for $0.50 |

4. Of the seven customers who visit your toy store, three spend $20, three spend $30, and one spends $22. What is the median amount that the customers spend?

   | | | |
   |---|---|---|
   | **A.** | ○ | $20 |
   | **B.** | ○ | $22 |
   | **C.** | ○ | $24 |
   | **D.** | ○ | $10 |

5. You work at a medical clinic where your job is to monitor people's weight. One patient has been weighed every Wednesday for two months. The recorded values of his weight (in pounds) are 180, 182, 181, 182, 184, 183, 182, and 182. What is the patient's mean weight according to this set of data?

| | | |
|---|---|---|
| A. | ○ | 181 lb |
| B. | ○ | 182 lb |
| C. | ○ | 183 lb |
| D. | ○ | 184 lb |

6. You work at a consumer product testing laboratory. You test two computer batteries and find that they each last for 3.0 hours before running out of power. Then you test a third battery. How long must it last for the mean running time to be 4.0 hours for the three batteries?

| | | |
|---|---|---|
| A. | ○ | 4.0 hr |
| B. | ○ | 5.0 hr |
| C. | ○ | 5.5 hr |
| D. | ○ | 6.0 hr |

7. You work at a television station. The ratings for the station's evening newscast are measured for seven nights in a row, from Sunday to Saturday. How can you determine the median rating?

| | | |
|---|---|---|
| A. | ○ | Add the ratings together, then divide by seven. |
| B. | ○ | Select the rating for Wednesday night. |
| C. | ○ | List the ratings in order from least to greatest, and select the fourth rating. |
| D. | ○ | Select the rating that is repeated most often. |

8. At a warehouse, the mean pay rate for all workers is $10.50 per hour. If your pay rate at the warehouse is $11.80 per hour, what can you conclude about the pay rates of the other workers?

| | | |
|---|---|---|
| A. | ○ | At least one of the other workers earns $10.50 per hour. |
| B. | ○ | At least one of the other workers earns less than $10.50 per hour. |
| C. | ○ | At least one of the other workers earns more than $10.50 per hour. |
| D. | ○ | Every worker works at a unique pay rate. |

Check your answers on page 157.

# Interpret Charts and Tables

## Build on What You Know

The data you need to complete a task may often be set in a chart or table. You have likely used charts and tables to organize information. Charts and tables present related data in an organized way. You might use charts and tables to compare different brands of washing machines, the costs of goods and services from different vendors, or the weather in different cities.

**Essential Tasks**

**Use** informal proportional reasoning strategies (e.g., **tables,** diagrams) **to solve problems**

**Create simple expressions or formulas** from real-life situations or **from tables**

### In Real Life    The Driver's Log

You work for a limousine service. The owner is concerned that some of the drivers do not understand the company's rates. The drivers should charge a few favored customers, including Key Medical and Cole Accounting, a discounted rate of $2.40 per mile. They should charge all other customers the standard rate of $2.80 per mile.

You decide to review the drivers' logs, which are the records they keep of their trips. Part of the log for one driver is shown below.

| Accounts | Budgets | Invoices | Print | | Refresh |

| Driver's Log | | | Driver: G. Brock | | |
| --- | --- | --- | --- | --- | --- |
| Date | Customer | Rate | Destination | Fare |
| 10/1 | Key Medical | $2.40/mile | Airport | $72.00 |
| 10/2 | Smith Legal | $2.80/mile | Airport | $100.80 |
| 10/2 | Best, Mr. Joseph | $2.80/mile | Downtown | $67.20 |
| 10/3 | Kiernan, Dr. Reg | $2.80/mile | 1983 Ireland St. | $95.20 |
| 10/3 | First National Bank | $2.40/mile | Airport | $86.80 |
| 10/4 | First National Bank | $2.80/mile | 76 Taylor Rd. | $70.00 |
| 10/5 | Cole Accounting | $2.40/mile | Airport | $88.80 |

 **With a classmate, discuss the following questions. Share your ideas with the class.**

1. Did the driver charge all of the customers the correct rate? Explain.

2. Can you tell if the driver charged Smith Legal correctly? If not, what additional information would be useful?

**Teacher Reminder**
Review the teacher lesson at
www.mysteckvaughn.com/WORK

**122** Math

# Using Headings

To analyze the data in a chart or table, begin by reading the title, column, and row headings. In many cases, only some of the columns or rows apply to the task you are completing. In the case of the driver's log for the limousine service, you needed to apply the information from the owner to two columns in the log: the columns for customer and rate. The data in the columns show that the driver charged First National Bank two different rates. Only one of those rates could be correct.

Sometimes a chart or table lacks important information that would help you analyze the data it presents. In the example of the limousine service, it would be helpful to have a complete list of the favored customers who should be charged the discounted rate. Without this list, you cannot tell if customers such as Smith Legal were charged correctly.

## In Real Life | The Doctors' Day

You schedule appointments at a medical office. The chart below shows the doctors' appointments for tomorrow from 9:00 A.M. to 1:00 P.M., when the office closes for the day. Each box in the chart represents a half-hour appointment. Arrows are used to show longer appointments. For example, M. Cready will see Dr. Crotty from 9:00 A.M. to 9:30 A.M. H. Gass will see Dr. Reubens from 11:00 A.M. to 12:30 P.M.

| Appointment Calendar | | | | |
|---|---|---|---|---|
| Time | Dr. Crotty | Dr. Kane | Dr. Reubens | Dr. Ward |
| 9:00 A.M. | M. Cready | N. Young | D. Appleman | T. North |
| | C. Doherty | [open] | T. Desnick | ↓ |
| 10:00 A.M. | ↓ | [open] | ↓ | M. Sinai |
| | ↓ | A. Brennan | [open] | ↓ |
| 11:00 A.M. | [open] | ↓ | H. Gass | A. Park |
| | C. Chung | ↓ | ↓ | ↓ |
| 12:00 P.M. | J. Horner | B. King | ↓ | [open] |
| | ↓ | ↓ | M. Loehman | [open] |

 **With a classmate, discuss the following questions. Share your ideas with the class.**

3. Mr. Tyler North calls and asks if he can change his appointment with Dr. Ward for later in the day. How do you respond?

4. Dr. Kane tells you that she may need 1 hour and 45 minutes with Andy Brennan. What do you suggest?

**Workplace Tip**

Customers or clients sometimes make requests that you cannot or should not grant. Always be polite while following the policies and rules of your company.

# Develop Your Skills

As you analyze the data in charts and tables, follow these steps:

- Read the title of the chart or table and the column and row headings. They will tell you the type of information in the chart or table and how that data is organized.
- Identify the data that you need to answer the question or solve a problem. Often you will need to study only a small amount of the data presented in a large chart or table.
- A chart or table may not present all of the facts and information you need. Identify if any needed information is missing. See if you can determine where you might be able to find that information. Apply facts from other sources if necessary.
- If the question or problem requires it, perform math operations (addition, subtraction, multiplication, and division) on the data.

## Finding the Lowest Price

A new manager at your company has chosen a set of furniture for her office. Your job is to purchase the furniture from one of three vendors: Abe's Place, Office Pro, and Super Mart. Each of these vendors sells the models that the manager has chosen. The prices are shown in the table.

| Cost of Furniture | | | | |
|---|---|---|---|---|
| Item | Model No. | Abe's Place | Office Pro | Super Mart |
| Chair | CH-294 | $255 | $280 | $290 |
| Desk | DK-010 | $1,200 | $1,090 | $1,286 |
| File Cabinet | FC-662 | $108 | $123 | $89 |
| Bookcase | BC-91X | $355 | $390 | $341 |

**Example:**

How can you determine which vendor offers the lowest price for the chair, desk, file cabinet, and bookcase? What is the lowest price for the four items? *Add the four prices in each column. The lowest price is $1,883 from Office Pro.*

**Example:**

When you call the customer service representative at Abe's Place, he tells you that his company offers free delivery on all orders over $1,000. What information should you get next to help you find the lowest price for your company? *the delivery charges of the other vendors*

**Example:**

The owner of your company asks you to order nine additional chairs (model CH-294) for the conference room. What is the lowest price for the total order? *$4,213 from Abe's Place*

**Missing Information**

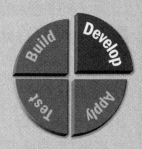

You manage accounts for Central City Plumbing, a company that sends plumbers to people's homes. The data table below shows one week of calls for the company. Some of the financial information is missing, however, as indicated by dashed lines.

| Service Calls for Central City Plumbing | | | | | | | | |
|---|---|---|---|---|---|---|---|---|
| Date | Customer | Plumber | Rate (Per Hour) | Arrive | Depart | Labor | Parts | Total Cost |
| 7/1 | F. Monroe 186 Main St | JB | $50.00 | 8:00 A.M. | 9:30 A.M. | $75.00 | $140.00 | $215.00 |
| 7/12 | O. Morris 71 Valley Rd | MK | $58.00 | 1:00 P.M. | 3:00 P.M. | $116.00 | $92.50 | $208.50 |
| 7/13 | E. Kopak 52 Kent Lane | JB | $50.00 | 1:30 P.M. | 2:00 P.M. | $25.00 | $43.00 | $68.00 |
| 7/14 | Peters Apps 20 Monroe St | FA | $62.00 | 3:00 P.M. | 4:30 P.M. | $93.00 | $83.25 | —— |
| 7/14 | H. Nusbaum 513 River Rd | MK | $58.00 | 3:00 P.M. | 5:00 P.M. | $116.00 | —— | $183.75 |
| 7/15 | W. Smith 41 Sunset Bl | FA | $62.00 | 9:00 A.M. | 11:30 A.M. | —— | $23.50 | $178.50 |
| 7/16 | S. Knutson 220 Park Ave | JB | $50.00 | 1:30 P.M. | 2:30 P.M. | —— | $64.25 | —— |

 **Use the table to answer these questions.**

1. Why do you think that the company charges three different rates for plumbing?

2. Why do you think the customers are identified by name and address, while the plumbers are identified only by their initials?

3. For each customer, how is the cost of labor calculated? How is the total cost calculated?

4. Calculate the missing data in the table.

---

**GOT IT?** To find and analyze information that is presented in charts and tables, you should:

- Read the title and column and row headings carefully.

- Apply important facts and information that are not included in the table.

- Perform mathematical operations when necessary.

**Answer Key**

1. Each plumber works at a different rate.

2. The company has many customers, while it employs only a few plumbers. The plumbers' full names may be listed elsewhere.

3. The cost of labor is the plumber's hourly rate mulitplied by the number of hours spent on the job. Add the cost of labor and parts to find the total cost.

4. Row 4: $176.25; Row 5: $67.75; Row 6: $155.00; Row 7: $50.00, $114.25

- ❏ **Read the title, column, and row headings.**
- ❏ **Choose which parts of the chart or table you need to solve the problem.**
- ❏ **Find and apply any information not presented in the chart or table as needed.**

# Apply Your Knowledge

The same types of charts and tables are used in a wide variety of jobs. Use the skills you have just learned to solve these problems.

**Read each of the following scenarios and examine the data presented in the table. Select the correct response for each question.**

Your company, based in Boston, is sending managers to Miami for a meeting. The Miami area is served by Miami International Airport (MIA) and an airport in Fort Lauderdale (FLL), a nearby city. You consult a reservation site on the Internet and find the flight information shown in the chart.

| Daily Flights from Boston to Miami Area | | | | | |
|---|---|---|---|---|---|
| Airline | Flight Number | Departs Boston (EST)* | Arrival Time (EST)* | Arrival Airport | Stops |
| National | 513 | 10:00 A.M. | 1:30 P.M. | MIA | nonstop |
| Eastern | 20 | 11:15 A.M. | 2:45 P.M. | FLL | nonstop |
| Air Red | 52 | 12:15 P.M. | 5:50 P.M. | MIA | Atlanta |
| National | 71 | 1:45 P.M. | 5:20 P.M. | FLL | nonstop |
| Air Red | 156 | 3:00 P.M. | 11:35 P.M. | MIA | Washington, Charlotte |
| Air Red | 1986 | 4:30 P.M. | 9:15 P.M. | MIA | Atlanta |
| Eastern | 2010 | 4:30 P.M. | 8:00 P.M. | MIA | nonstop |
| Gold Air | 8 | 6:00 P.M. | 11:28 P.M. | FLL | Orlando |

*Eastern Standard Time

1. One manager would like to depart sometime after 2:30 P.M. and arrive as early as possible at any Miami area airport. Which flight best meets these needs?

   A. National flight 71

   B. Air Red flight 156

   C. Air Red flight 1986

   D. Eastern flight 2010

2. The company owner directs you to purchase a ticket in his name for a morning flight to Fort Lauderdale on National Airlines. How should you respond?

   A. Purchase a ticket for the owner on National flight 513.

   B. Purchase a ticket for the owner on National flight 71.

   C. Purchase a ticket for the owner on Eastern flight 20.

   D. Tell the owner that you can meet two of his requests, but not all three.

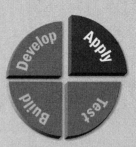

3. To whom would you recommend Gold Air flight 8?

   A. someone who must work a full day in the Boston office

   B. someone who prefers to fly to the Mlami airport

   C. someone who would like to visit downtown Orlando

   D. someone who prefers not to fly Air Red

4. Which is a typical flying time for a Boston to Miami nonstop flight?

   A. 2 hr, 30 min

   B. 3 hr, 30 min

   C. 5 hr, 30 min

   D. 8 hr

## In Real Life  Put Your Skills to Work!

You are ordering paving stones for a construction project. You research the cost from three vendors and record the data in the chart.

| Cost of Paving Stones | | |
|---|---|---|
| Vendor | Price | Delivery Charge |
| Bob's Depot | $3.50 per stone | $120 per order |
| BrickMart | $4.00 per stone | $80 per order |
| Home Value | $4.80 per stone | (free) |

 **Think about the problem you are facing and put your skills to work! When ordering different amounts of stone, how might the lowest total price change? Experiment with various amounts of stones.**

## Think About It!

**Why are charts and tables useful for presenting data?**

**Why are computers often used to keep data in a chart or table?**

Charts and tables help organize data sets. Some charts and tables have as few as two columns, others may have dozens of columns and hundreds of rows. In many jobs, computers are used to store and present large charts and tables. Computers are excellent tools for tracking information and performing calculations on numerical data. But whether a chart or table is presented on a computer screen or paper, you still need to apply the same skills to make sense of the data.

**Answer Key**

1. D
2. D
3. A
4. B

# Test Your WRC Skills

**Solving mathematical problems requires that you use different problem-solving strategies. Read the following situations. Select which answer you think is the correct response.**

1. The table below shows a driver's log for a limousine service.

| Date | Customer | Rate | Miles | Tolls | Charge |
|------|----------|------|-------|-------|--------|
| 3/10 | Key Medical | $2.40/mile | 80 | $2.00 | $194.00 |
| 3/10 | Cole Accounting | $2.40/mile | 35 | $0 | $84.00 |
| 3/11 | Burns, Mr. Wm | $2.80/mile | 18 | $1.20 | $51.60 |
| 3/12 | Key Medical | $2.40/mile | 33 | $1.20 | $80.40 |
| 3/12 | First National Bank | $2.80/mile | 38 | $0 | $106.40 |
| 3/13 | First National Bank | $2.80/mile | 49 | $4.00 | $141.20 |
| 3/15 | Cole Accounting | $2.40/mile | 25 | $2.00 | $62.00 |

Which formula could you use to calculate the charge for a customer's trip?

A. ◯    Miles + Tolls

B. ◯    Rate × (Miles + Tolls)

C. ◯    (Rate × Miles) + Tolls

D. ◯    (Rate ÷ Miles) + Tolls

2. According to the table, Cole Accounting used the service on 3/10 and 3/15. What were the total charges for Cole Accounting for those two days?

A. ◯    $84.00

B. ◯    $146.00

C. ◯    $62.00

D. ◯    $194.00

3. On 3/13, First National Bank was charged $2.80 per mile for a 49-mile trip. How much money would First National Bank have saved had they been charged a rate of $2.40 per mile on that trip?

A. ◯    $19.60

B. ◯    $23.60

C. ◯    $34.80

D. ◯    $117.60

The chart below shows the stations and departure times for four commuter trains. A dash shows that the train skips a station. Use the chart to answer questions 4 and 5.

| Train | Downtown | 18th St. | Yardley | W. Haven | Irish Hill | Kiernan | Regina |
|-------|----------|----------|---------|----------|------------|---------|--------|
| 34 | 5:10 P.M. | 5:25 P.M. | 5:39 P.M. | 5:48 P.M. | 5:55 P.M. | 6:01 P.M. | 6:10 P.M. |
| 6 | 5:40 P.M. | 5:55 P.M. | — | — | — | 6:20 P.M. | 6:30 P.M. |
| 14 | 6:00 P.M. | 6:15 P.M. | 6:29 P.M. | 6:38 P.M. | — | — | — |
| 29 | 6:15 P.M. | 6:30 P.M. | — | — | 6:55 P.M. | 7:01 P.M. | 7:10 P.M. |

4. Which train is scheduled to travel from Downtown to the Regina Station in the shortest amount of time?

A. ◯ Train 34
B. ◯ Train 6
C. ◯ Train 14
D. ◯ Train 29

5. Your office is a 15-minute walk from the 18th Street Station. When is the latest time you can leave work, board a train at 18th Street, and arrive at Kiernan Station at 6:20 P.M.?

A. ◯ 5:40 P.M.
B. ◯ 5:45 P.M.
C. ◯ 5:10 P.M.
D. ◯ 4:55 P.M.

6. You help buy equipment at a school. The science teacher asks you to buy a set of 90 microscope slides. The table below shows prices from four vendors. Which order meets the teacher's request and has the lowest price? (Ignore charges for tax and shipping.)

| Vendor | Cost Per Package | Number of Slides Per Package |
|--------|------------------|------------------------------|
| Eimer Biological | $26.40 | 30 slides |
| Maryland Scientific | $76.50 | 90 slides |
| JSB Supplies | $55.20 | 60 slides |
| Kane School Supply | $39.00 | 45 slides |

A. ◯ 2 packages from Kane School Supply
B. ◯ 3 packages from Eimer Biological
C. ◯ 1 package from JSB Supplies and 1 package from Eimer Biological
D. ◯ 1 package from Maryland Scientific

Check your answers on page 158.

# Compare and Contrast Data

## Build on What You Know

When working with data, it is important that you can assess whether or not the data is reliable. Reliable sets of data correctly reflect their sources. Examples of data sets that are generally reliable include bank statements and product information from trusted manufacturers.

Many factors can make data less reliable. Sometimes people make mistakes when they record data. Sometimes people let their opinions affect the data they record. People also can misinterpret data, meaning they do not draw accurate conclusions. Evaluating the reliability of data is an important skill.

### In Real Life  Simon's Survey: Part 1

A flower shop owner is curious about her customers' opinions. She asks Simon, a manager, to conduct a survey. During one afternoon, Simon asks the customers to rate the flower shop in four categories: quality of the flowers, speed of service, value, and overall experience. The best rating is 10 and the worst is 1. The results are shown below.

| Customer | Quality | Speed | Value | Overall |
|---|---|---|---|---|
| A | 10 | 2 | 7 | 8 |
| B | 9 | 5 | 7 | 6 |
| C | 10 | 10 | 6 | 9 |
| D | 8 | 3 | 6 | 6 |
| E | 9 | 2 | 8 | 9 |
| F | 9 | 2 | 8 | 8 |
| G | 8 | 8 | 9 | 0 |
| **Mean** | 9.0 | 4.6 | 7.3 | 6.6 |

**With a classmate, discuss the following questions. Share your ideas with the class.**

1. How are the responses for the speed of service different from the responses for the other categories?

2. Do you doubt the reliability of any of the entries? Explain.

3. What conclusions can you draw from the survey? What additional data would help you reach stronger conclusions?

### Workplace Tip

You always need to use common sense. Question facts or data that you do not think are correct.

**Teacher Reminder**
Review the teacher lesson at
www.mysteckvaughn.com/WORK

**130** Math

# Analyzing a Survey

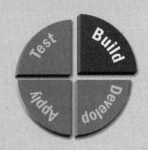

Businesses often distribute surveys to learn what their customers—or potential customers—are thinking. As a general rule, the more people that take the survey, the more accurate and useful are the results. But many factors can distort the results of a survey. In the case of Simon's survey, he may have conducted it when one of the florists was sick and service was unusually slow. Or perhaps that day's customers were not typical. For a survey's results to be useful, the participants should represent a large group of people, such as all the customers over a longer period of time.

When you analyze a survey, pay attention to the ranges of the responses. In Simon's survey, customers rated the quality over a narrow range from 8 to 10. In contrast, the ratings for speed of service covered a wide range, from 2 to 10. These are differences in **variability**, a measure of the distribution of a set of data. Data that falls mostly within a narrow range has low variability, while widely spread data is described as highly variable. **Variance** is a common measurement of variability.

Did you notice the entry of 0 for overall experience, even when the ratings were meant to be from 1 to 10? This rating is an example of an **outlier**, a data entry that falls outside the typical range. You often can discount or ignore the outliers in a survey because they do not reflect typical opinions. In this case, the outlier may have been entered incorrectly.

## In Real Life   Simon's Survey: Part 2

For the rest of the week during his shift, Simon continues to ask customers to respond to his survey. He surveys 100 customers and reports the following data.

|          | Quality | Speed | Value | Overall |
|----------|---------|-------|-------|---------|
| **Mean**     | 8.9     | 6.3   | 7.5   | 6.9     |
| **Variance** | 0.2     | 2.1   | 0.3   | 0.4     |

 **With a classmate, discuss the following questions. Share your ideas with the class.**

4. Why are the results from Part 2 of the survey more useful than the results from Part 1?

5. How do the mean results for the four categories compare between Part 1 and Part 2?

6. The variance was much higher for speed than for the other three categories. What might this mean?

# Develop Your Skills

Remember that data is not always reliable, and that even reliable data can be misinterpreted. When you evaluate data, consider how it was obtained. This will help you figure out what the data means. You also need to use common sense to identify false data or recognize an unlikely conclusion.

## In Real Life    The Pizza Survey

You are helping the owner of Mike's Pizzeria evaluate the results of three different surveys. In each survey, people were asked to choose their favorite pizza parlor. The results are shown in the circle graphs.

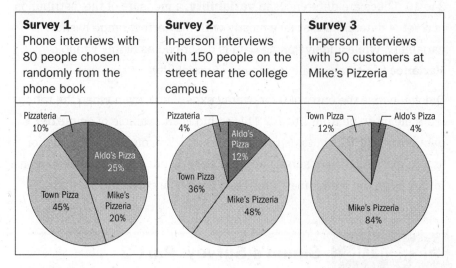

**Survey 1**
Phone interviews with 80 people chosen randomly from the phone book

**Survey 2**
In-person interviews with 150 people on the street near the college campus

**Survey 3**
In-person interviews with 50 customers at Mike's Pizzeria

Key: ■ Aldo's Pizza  ▨ Mike's Pizzeria  ▨ Town Pizza  ■ Pizzateria

 **Look closely at the three circle graphs and at the key. Then discuss these questions. Share your ideas with the class.**

1. Which survey do you think most accurately reflects the opinions of the people in town? Explain.

2. Compare the results of Survey 2 with Survey 1. What do they show about the people who prefer Mike's Pizzeria?

3. Why do you think Mike's Pizzeria was so popular in Survey 3?

## Probability

Surveys can also be used to calculate **probability**, which is the likelihood that an event will occur. For example, the results of Survey 1 suggest that 20% of the townspeople prefer Mike's Pizzeria. If this is true, then if a random person in town is chosen, there is a probability of 20% that Mike's Pizzeria is that person's favorite. Probability can also be expressed as a fraction. A probability of 20% equals $\frac{20}{100}$ or $\frac{1}{5}$.

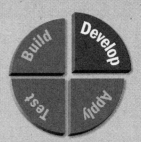

## In Real Life  The Auto Dealership

You work for an auto dealership that sells pre-owned cars. To gather data about the business, you choose ten customers at random. You organize the data you collected in the table below.

| Data from Ten Randomly Chosen Buyers of Pre-Owned Cars | | | | | |
|---|---|---|---|---|---|
| Customer | Model | Year | Color | Mileage | Price |
| F. Hogan | sedan | 2005 | red | 35,000 | $10,950 |
| B. Bird | sedan | 2008 | white | 23,100 | $12,030 |
| W. Heaton | SUV | 2003 | white | 98,900 | $3,350 |
| A. Kiner | coupe | 2009 | blue | 10,400 | $20,430 |
| R. Boone | pick-up truck | 2007 | blue | 45,900 | $9,110 |
| C. Lao | hatchback | 2003 | black | 89,300 | $3,880 |
| J. Manship | sedan | 2001 | black | 105,200 | $3,200 |
| E. Dolan | sedan | 2000 | blue | 119,400 | $3,450 |
| F. Smith | coupe | 2007 | white | 67,800 | $9,410 |
| R. Gold | pick-up truck | 2009 | red | 12,500 | $15,400 |

**Example:**

If the ten customers in the table accurately represent the dealership's customers, what is the probability that a car purchase is for a white car? *In the table, three out of the ten cars are white. The probability of a white car being purchased is $\frac{3}{10}$, or 30%.*

**Example:**

Are the prices of pre-owned cars determined more by model than by mileage? Explain. *Compare the data in the columns for Model and Price, then for Mileage and Price. Sedans sold for about $3,000 to more than $10,000. Cars with low mileage sold for more than cars with high mileage. This shows that price depends more on mileage than on model.*

## GOT IT?  When you evaluate data from different sources, you should:

- Determine how the data was obtained.

- Consider the reliability of the data and its source.

- Compare and contrast different sets of data to draw the most useful conclusions about them.

# Apply Your Knowledge

You need to evaluate data in a wide variety of jobs. Use the skills you have just learned to solve these problems.

**Use the information below to answer questions 1 and 2.**

You work at MKB Gardens, a store that sells plants, gardening supplies, and related merchandise. Your manager is concerned that the store's prices are significantly higher than prices at three competing stores. To test this idea, you choose five representative products sold at all four stores. You learn the competitors' prices by asking clerks over the telephone. Your results are shown in the table.

| Store | Rose Bush | Juniper Shrub (1 ft tall) | Seeds (Standard Package) | Garden Fertilizer (15 lb bag) | Firewood (20 lb) |
|---|---|---|---|---|---|
| MKB Gardens | $4.99 | $19.45 | $1.00 | $25.75 | $6.00 |
| Fran's Home & Garden | $6.60 | $18.00 | $0.85 | $29.95 | $4.50 |
| Aiden's Acre | $5.50 | $15.00 | $0.75 | $28.50 | $7.00 |
| F & A Gardens | $4.80 | $101.50 | $1.25 | $31.00 | $7.50 |
| **Mean** | $5.47 | $38.49 | $0.96 | $28.80 | $6.25 |

1. Which entry in the table is an outlier that is most likely incorrect?

   A. the price of a rose bush at MKB Gardens

   B. the price of garden fertilizer at F & A Gardens

   C. the price of firewood at Fran's Home & Garden

   D. the price of a juniper shrub at F & A Gardens

2. What can be reasonably concluded from the data in the table?

   A. Prices are significantly higher at MKB Gardens than at its competitors.

   B. Prices are similar at the four stores, and none has consistently lower prices.

   C. Price differences at the four stores are due to differences in quality of the products.

   D. MKB Gardens should match the lowest prices of its competitors.

3. You stock vending machines in office buildings throughout the city. You have a choice of four different brands of potato chips to sell in the machines. Each brand has a similar cost. You decide to conduct a taste test among potential customers to determine which brand to sell.

With the proper permission, where would be the most useful place to conduct the taste test?

**A.** at a supermarket or shopping mall

**B.** at an office building where the vending machines are popular

**C.** at a cafeteria where potato chips are not served

**D.** at the cafeteria where you and your coworkers eat lunch

## In Real Life  Put Your Skills to Work!

At the factory where you work, the manager believes that most of the 150 employees are arriving late for the 9:00 A.M. shift. The data table shows the arrival times of three employees over one workweek in February.

| Employee | 2/3 | 2/4 | 2/5 | 2/6 | 2/7 |
|---|---|---|---|---|---|
| A | 9:00 | 9:04 | 8:59 | 10:45 | 8:58 |
| B | 9:20 | 9:15 | 9:14 | 9:18 | 9:15 |
| C | 8:45 | 9:32 | 9:38 | 9:08 | 8:58 |

 **Think about the problem you are facing and put your skills to work! Which time entry is an outlier, and what might have caused it? Which employee has the greatest variance, or variability, of arrival times? Does the data support the manager's belief that most employees are arriving late?**

**Workplace Tip**

When answering the questions, did you:

- determine how the data was obtained?
- compare all the data entries that were relevant?
- use what you know and your common sense to determine if the data were reliable?

## Think About It!

Why are some data sets more reliable and useful than others?

Why can it be difficult to draw conclusions from a small sample of data?

What do mean and variability tell you about a data set?

Remember that the usefulness of data depends on many factors, including the source of the data and the accuracy of the data collector. Avoid drawing conclusions or making predictions that a set of data does not support.

**Answer Key**

1. D

2. B

3. B

# Test Your WRC Skills

**Solving mathematical problems requires that you use different problem-solving strategies. Read the following situations. Select which answer you think is the correct response.**

**1.** You are the host at a restaurant. One evening you choose seven tables at random to receive a customer-satisfaction survey. The survey asks customers to rate the restaurant on a scale from 1 (low) to 10 (high) in three categories: quality of the food, quality of the service, and value. The results of your survey are shown in the table below.

| Table | Waiter/ Waitress | Size of Party | Food | Service | Value |
|-------|------------------|---------------|------|---------|-------|
| A | PB | 3 | 5 | 9 | 2 |
| B | MC | 2 | 7 | 9 | 5 |
| C | AL | 3 | 6 | 10 | 9 |
| D | MC | 2 | 5 | 8 | 3 |
| E | PB | 6 | 7 | 9 | 7 |
| F | PB | 4 | 6 | 8 | 5 |
| G | AL | 2 | 6 | 8 | 8 |
| **Mean** | | 3.1 | 6.0 | 8.7 | 5.6 |

Which category of data has the greatest variability?

| A. | ○ | Size of Party |
|----|----|---------------|
| B. | ○ | Food |
| C. | ○ | Service |
| D. | ○ | Value |

**2.** Based on the data, how does the customer's rating for service relate to the size of the party at the table?

| A. | ○ | High service ratings are more likely from larger parties. |
|----|----|-----------------------------------------------------------|
| B. | ○ | High service ratings are more likely from smaller parties. |
| C. | ○ | High service ratings are more likely from families with two or more children. |
| D. | ○ | Service ratings are unrelated to the size of the party. |

**3.** Which would produce data that best represents all of the restaurants' customers?

| A. | ○ | giving the survey to many customers over one week |
|----|----|----------------------------------------------------|
| B. | ○ | changing the rating scale from 1 to 5 |
| C. | ○ | giving the survey only to familiar or favorite customers |
| D. | ○ | giving the survey only to customers of the best waiter or waitress |

4.  You help manage a parking lot for commuters. The owner suggests raising the daily parking fee from $8 to $12. To predict the effect of the rate increase, you survey 20 customers who pay the daily rate. The results are shown below.

| What would you do if the lot increased its fee to $12 per day? | Number of Responses | Percentage |
| --- | --- | --- |
| Park here about as often as always | 9 | 45% |
| Park here about half as often | 6 | 30% |
| Switch to a less expensive lot | 4 | 20% |
| Don't know or no response | 1 | 5% |
| TOTAL | 20 | 100% |

Which fact about the survey, if true, would decrease the reliability of the data?

| A. | ○ | More men than women are daily customers of the parking lot. |
| B. | ○ | The customers in the survey were chosen randomly during the week. |
| C. | ○ | Of the 20 responses, 3 were from the same customer. |
| D. | ○ | Of the 20 responses, 3 were from first-time customers. |

5.  Based on the survey, what is the most likely effect of the new rate?

| A. | ○ | The lot will lose about $\frac{1}{3}$ of its daily customers. |
| B. | ○ | The lot will lose more than $\frac{1}{2}$ of its daily customers. |
| C. | ○ | The lot will gain daily customers. |
| D. | ○ | The lot will lose between 4 and 8 customers. |

6.  You sell insurance policies over the telephone. Your manager tells you that company surveys show that 25 of 100 people called will be interested in the policy. If this is true, what is the probability that the next person you call will be interested in the policy?

| A. | ○ | $\frac{1}{5}$ |
| B. | ○ | $\frac{1}{4}$ |
| C. | ○ | $\frac{1}{3}$ |
| D. | ○ | $\frac{1}{7}$ |

Check your answers on page 159.

# Skills for the Workplace

## Create a Table

Presenting data in tables makes it easier to read and quicker to find what you are looking for. Sometimes you will be presented with data and expected to use it to generate a table or chart. You may also work with spreadsheet software, which is a program that helps you organize data into tables. Before you begin organizing data into a table, answer the following questions.

- What will the title be?
- What are the different categories of data?
- How is the data measured? What units are used?
- What will your row and/or column headings be?

## Workplace Scenario

You are working as a clerk at a car dealership. Your supervisor has e-mailed you the monthly sales figures, as shown below.

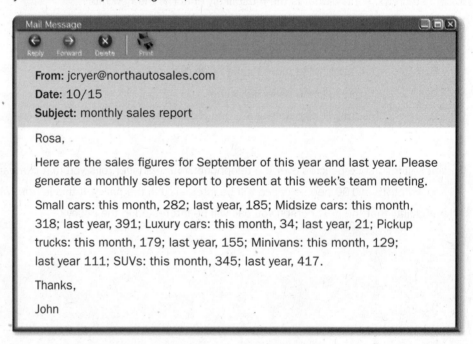

**Mail Message**

Reply  Forward  Delete  Print

**From:** jcryer@northautosales.com
**Date:** 10/15
**Subject:** monthly sales report

Rosa,

Here are the sales figures for September of this year and last year. Please generate a monthly sales report to present at this week's team meeting.

Small cars: this month, 282; last year, 185; Midsize cars: this month, 318; last year, 391; Luxury cars: this month, 34; last year, 21; Pickup trucks: this month, 179; last year, 155; Minivans: this month, 129; last year 111; SUVs: this month, 345; last year, 417.

Thanks,

John

- What will you title your table? *Monthly Sales Figures Comparison*
- What are the different categories of data? *small cars, midsize cars, luxury cars, pickup trucks, minivans, and SUVs*
- What units are used for the data? *number of vehicles*
- What will your column and row headings be? *The column heads will be Vehicle Type; September sales this year; September sales last year. The row headings will be each category of data.*
- How many columns and rows do you need? *three columns; seven rows.*

> ### Workplace Tip
> Remember that you need to account for the row and column headings when determining the number of columns and rows that you will need for your table.

# Workplace Practice

Use the sales data in the e-mail to create the table.

| Monthly Sales Figures Comparison | | |
|---|---|---|
| Vehicle type | September sales this year | September sales last year |
| Small cars | 282 | 185 |
| Midsize cars | 318 | 391 |
| Luxury cars | 34 | 21 |
| Pickup trucks | 179 | 155 |
| Minivans | 129 | 111 |
| SUVs | 345 | 417 |

- Which vehicle types showed an increase in sales from last year? *small cars, luxury cars, pickup trucks, minivans*

- Which vehicle types showed a decrease in sales from last year? *midsize cars and SUVs*

- How did the table help you to answer the questions above? *The information was organized, which made it easier to compare the data side by side.*

## It's Your Turn!

Your boss gives you the following information on employee work hours for the next week and asks you to make a table showing which employees are working on each day. The shifts are from 8:00 A.M. to 4:00 P.M. and 3:00 P.M. to 11:00 P.M.

**Amir:** early shift Monday–Friday

**Mallory:** late shift Monday, Wednesday, Friday; early shift Tuesday, Thursday

**Fredo:** early shift Monday–Wednesday; late shift Thursday, Friday

**Ravi:** late shift Monday, Tuesday; early shift Wednesday–Friday

**Jessica:** late shift Monday–Friday

**Chen:** early shift Monday, Friday; late shift Tuesday–Thursday

1. What will you title your table?

2. What are the different categories of data?

3. What will your column and row headings be?

4. How many columns and rows do you need?

5. On a separate piece of paper, make your table.

**Answer Key**

*Sample answers:*

**1.** Work Schedule, Week of 10/18

**2.** days of the week; early and late shift

**3.** Column headings: Day; Shift; Early Shift; Late Shift
Row headings: Monday; Tuesday; Wednesday; Thursday; Friday

**4.** three columns; seven rows

**5.** Sample table:

| Day | Shift | |
|---|---|---|
| | Early Shift | Late Shift |
| Monday | Amir Fredo Chen | Mallory Jessica Ravi |
| Tuesday | Amir Mallory Fredo | Ravi Jessica Chen |
| Wednesday | Amir Fredo Ravi | Mallory Jessica Chen |
| Thursday | Amir Mallory Ravi | Fredo Jessica Chen |
| Friday | Amir Ravi Chen | Mallory Fredo Jessica |

# Chapter 4 Assessment

**Read each problem and choose the best answer.**

1. A carpenter has eight wooden boards. The table shows the lengths of the boards.

| Board Lengths | 41.2 cm | 41.0 cm | 41.7 cm | 40.9 cm | 41.1 cm | 40.8 cm | 40.3 cm | 41.0 cm |
|---|---|---|---|---|---|---|---|---|

What is the mean length of the boards?

A. ○ 41.0 cm

B. ○ 41.1 cm

C. ○ 40.9 cm

D. ○ 41.2 cm

2. Every month, a vendor delivers a case of copy-machine paper to your office. The vendor charges a different price depending on the manufacturer's cost. The table shows the cost of one ream of paper (500 sheets) over 8 months.

| Month | Jan. | Feb. | Mar. | Apr. | May | June | July | August |
|---|---|---|---|---|---|---|---|---|
| Cost of Paper (per Ream) | $5.80 | $5.85 | $5.80 | $5.80 | $5.60 | $5.80 | $5.85 | $5.75 |

Which set of terms describe the value of $5.80 for this data?

A. ○ mode and range

B. ○ mean and mode

C. ○ mean and median

D. ○ median and mode

3. You work at a pet-supply store. A customer wants to pay the lowest price per pound of dog food that does not contain fish. Which brand do you recommend?

| Dog Food | Weight | Ingredients | Price |
|---|---|---|---|
| Fran's Gourmet Dog Food | 30 lb | beef only, no grains | $61.20 |
| Whole Dog Cuisine | 18 lb | beef, lamb, chicken, corn | $46.00 |
| MKB Dog Food | 20 lb | beef, poultry, fish | $39.50 |
| River Road Dog Food | 12 lb | turkey, lamb, duck | $37.75 |

A. ○ Fran's Gourmet Dog Food

B. ○ Whole Dog Cuisine

C. ○ MKB Dog Food

D. ○ River Road Dog Food

4. You sell lift tickets at a ski area. Skiers can buy a lift ticket for 1, 2, or 4 days of skiing, and children are charged less than adults. The prices (including tax) are shown in the chart.

| Days | Adult Lift Ticket | Child Lift Ticket (age 3–5) | Child Lift Ticket (age 6–14) |
|------|-------------------|-----------------------------|------------------------------|
| 1 | $50.00 | $20.00 | $30.00 |
| 2 | $90.00 | $35.00 | $55.00 |
| 4 | $160.00 | $60.00 | $90.00 |

How much money is saved by a family of 4 (two adults, one 4-year-old, and one 12-year-old) that buys a 4-day ticket for each family member instead of four 1-day tickets?

A. ○ $40.00
B. ○ $80.00
C. ○ $130.00
D. ○ $150.00

5. The table shows five customer responses to a survey about your home-cleaning service. Each customer was asked to rate his or her experience on a scale from 1 (poorest) to 10 (best).

| Rating of service | 9 | 8 | 10 | 2 | 8 | Mean: 7.4 |
|-------------------|---|---|----|---|---|-----------|

Which would help you determine whether the mean rating truly reflects customers' opinions?

A. ○ Eliminate the rating of 2 and re-calculate the mean.
B. ○ Change the rating of 2 to a rating of 9 or 10.
C. ○ Interview the five customers who participated in the survey.
D. ○ Give the survey to many more customers.

6. You record all the orders taken during 1 hour at the ice cream shop where you work.

| Flavor | Chocolate | Vanilla | Strawberry | Pistachio | Rainbow | Mint Chip | Coffee |
|--------|-----------|---------|------------|-----------|---------|-----------|--------|
| Number of Orders | 5 | 4 | 4 | 3 | 2 | 1 | 1 |

Based on this data, and assuming each customer asks for one flavor only, what is the probability that a randomly-chosen customer will ask for strawberry ice cream?

A. ○ $\frac{1}{7}$
B. ○ $\frac{1}{5}$
C. ○ $\frac{4}{7}$
D. ○ $\frac{4}{1}$

For more Chapter 4 assessment questions, please visit www.mysteckvaughn.com/WORK

Check your answers on page 160.

# WorkSkills™ Glossary

The following words were used in the WorkSkills™ Math book. Knowing these words will help you as you study for the National Work Readiness Credential assessment.

## A

**Area** (**er**-ee-uh) the measure of the size of a surface

## B

**Budget** (**buh**-juht) amount of money that is allocated for a particular purpose

## C

**Capacity** (kuh-**pah**-suh-tee) the measure of how much an object can hold

**Circumference** (suh-**kuhm**-fuhrns) the distance around a circular figure

**Constant** (**kahn**-stuhnt) a value that does not change

**Convert** (kuhn-**vuhrt**) to change a measurement from one unit to another

**Customary measurement system** (**kuhs**-tuh-mer-ee **meh**-zhur-muhnt **sis**-tuhm) a measurement system with standard units used to measure length (or distance), weight, and capacity; used in the U.S.

## D

**Data** (**dey**-tuh) organized factual information

**Divide** (duh-**vahyd**) to find the quotient of

## E

**Equivalent** (ih-**kwiv**-luhnt) equal in value

**Estimate** (**es**-tuh-mayt) rough calculation or approximation

## Expression
**Expression** (ik-**spre**-shuhn) a relationship between mathematical terms that may contain numbers, operation symbols, and variables

## F

**Formula** (**for**-myuh-luh) an equation that represents a relationship between values

## I

**Irrelevant** (ih-**re**-luh-vuhnt) that which has no connection to a task or is not necessary to solve a problem

## L

**Length** (lenth) the measure of the distance between two points

## M

**Mean** (meen) the average of a set of data

**Median** (mee-dee-uhn) the middle value of a set of data

**Mode** (mohd) the value that appears most often in a set of data

**Multiply** (**muhl**-tih-plahy) to find the product of

## O

**Outlier** (**aut**-lahy-uhr) a data entry that falls outside the typical range in a set of data

**Order of operations** (**ohr**-duhr uhv ah-puh-**rey**-shuhns) the sequence of steps performed to solve a problem that involves addition, subtraction, multiplication, and/or division

## P

**Percent** (pur-**sent**) a ratio that tells you how many out of 100

**Perimeter** (puh-**rih**-muh-tuhr) the distance around a figure

**Probability** (prah-buh-**bi**-luh-tee) the likelihood that an event will occur

## R

**Range** (reynj) the difference in the least and greatest values of a set of data

**Ratio** (**rey**-shee-oh) the relationship between two amounts

**Reconcile** (**re**-kuhn-sahyl) to determine whether or not an amount is within a budget

**Relevant** (**re**-luh-vuhnt) that which is related or connected to the problem that you are trying to solve or the task you are trying to complete

**Round** (round) to increase or decrease a number based on a given place value

## S

**Strategy** (**strah**-tuh-jee) a plan that is developed in order to achieve a goal

## T

**Translate** (**trans**-leyt) to take information in a problem and change it into a math expression

## V

**Variability** (ver-ee-uh-**bi**-luh-tee) a measure of the distribution of a set of data

**Variance** (**ver**-ee-uhns) a common measurement of variability

**Volume** (**vahl**-yoom) the amount of space inside a three-dimensional figure

## W

**Weight** (weyt) the measure of how heavy something is

# Answers and Solutions

## Lesson 1 Test Your WRC Skills (pages 30–31)

**1. C. $1,174.00**
Option C is correct because you multiplied $0.50 by 2,348 miles and put the decimal point in the correct place. Options A and B are incorrect because you inserted the decimal point in the wrong place in the product. Option D is incorrect because you gave the total number of miles you drove as the total you would be reimbursed rather than multiplying that number by the amount you are reimbursed per mile.

**2. D. $216**
Option D is correct because you added the costs of the material, your labor, and your supplies to find the total amout you will charge the customer. Option A is incorrect because this is the total of your charge for labor and supplies—it does not include the material the customer selected. Option B is incorrect because it is the total cost of the material the customer selected only—it does not include your charges for labor and supplies. Option C is incorrect. This is the cost of the material the customer selected as well as your labor charge. It does not include the cost for your supplies.

**3. D. 11,520**
Option D is correct because you multiplied the number of boxes you received by the number of cans in each box. Option A is incorrect because you gave the number of cans in each box. Option B is incorrect because you added the number of boxes to the number of cans in each box instead of multiplying. Option C is incorrect because you multiplied 144 by 8 instead of 80 (the number of boxes received).

**4. C. $11.45**
Option C is correct because you added the cost of each item together to find the total cost. Option A is incorrect because you found the cost of only one hamburger, the order of fries, and only one drink. Option B is incorrect because you added the cost of two hamburgers, one order of fries, and only one drink. Option D is incorrect because you added an extra order of fries.

**5. C. 81**
Option C is correct. You multiplied the number of people in the meeting by the number of different handouts. Option A is incorrect because you divided instead of multiplying. Option B is incorrect because you added instead of multiplying. Option D is incorrect because you multiplied the number of people by three times as many handouts as there actually are.

**6. C. 150**
Option C is correct because you added the number of animals groomed for each of the four months. Option B is incorrect because you did not include the number of animals for one of the months of either June or July. Options A and D are incorrect because the numbers were not accurately added together.

**7. C. $600**
Option C is correct. You have saved $600, which is determined by multiplying the number of months you have been saving by the amount you have saved each month. Option A is incorrect because you subtracted the amount that you saved each month from the cost of the television. Option B is incorrect because you gave the cost of the television rather than the amount that you have saved. Option D is incorrect because you added the cost of the television to the amount that you saved for one month.

**8. D. $467.64**
Option D is correct. You multiplied the cost of one box by the number of boxes that Carlos need to order. Option A is incorrect because you gave the cost for one box of pens. Option B is incorrect because you multiplied 12 by 3 and then added the correct cost for one box ($12.99). Option C is incorrect because you multiplied the number of boxes Carlos needs to buy by $12.00 instead of $12.99.

# Lesson 2 Test Your WRC Skills (pages 38–39)

**1. C. the weight of each container**
Option C is correct because you need to add the weight of each container you have loaded onto the trailer to be sure that the trailer is not over the weight limit. Options A and D are incorrect because the volume and the color of each container is irrelevant. Option B is not correct because the number of containers that you can load onto the trailer depends on the weight of each container. You can only load containers onto the trailer until you have reached the weight limit.

**2. D. the number of gallons in each crate**
Option D is correct because you need to know how many gallons you need to fill the remaining shelves, and so how many crates you need to wheel in. To find this information, you need to multiply the number of gallons per shelf by the number of shelves left to be filled and then divide that product by the number of gallons in each crate. Options A and B are incorrect because the volume and the weight of each container is irrelevant. Option C is not correct because you already know the number of gallons that can fit on each shelf.

**3. A. the number of bags of mulch on each pallet**
Option A is correct because you need to divide the number of bags the nursery has requested by the number of bags of mulch on each pallet in order to figure out how many pallets you need to load onto the truck. Options B, C, and D are incorrect because the information is irrelevant to solving the problem.

**4. C. The delivery department has used 127 gallons of fuel for their delivery vans.**
Option C is correct because you have been asked to order office supplies, and the amount of fuel that the delivery department has used is not something that you will be required to purchase. Options A, B, and D are incorrect because these items are all office supplies, and so are things that your supervisor will expect you to order.

**5. B. how many encyclopedias will fit on the cart**
Option B is correct because you need to know the number of encyclopedias that can fit on the cart to figure out how many trips you need to take. Once you have determined how many books you can take on each trip, you can divide that number by the total number of encyclopedias to be moved to find the number of trips you need to take. Options A, C, and D are incorrect because the weight and the order of the encyclopedias, as well as the distance between the two shelves, is irrelevant.

**6. B. $125.00**
Option B is correct because it represents the monetary value of the product that the customer ordered, not any of the amounts that you collected on your route. Options A, C, and D are incorrect because they each represent an amount that you collected on your stops. To find the total collected for the day, you would add each of these amounts together.

**7. A. the number of lines at the factory**
Option A is correct because in order to find the total number of chairs assembled per shift, you need to multiply the number of chairs each line can assemble by the number of lines. Options B, C, and D are incorrect because they are irrelevant to solving the problem.

**8. B. the total square feet of wall that needs to be painted**
Option B is correct because you will need to know the square footage of one wall and multiply that number by 4 in order to determine the total square footage that needs to be painted. You need to know the total square footage being painted in order to determine how much paint to buy. Options A, C, and D are incorrect because they are irrelevant to solving the problem. None of that information will affect the amount of paint that needs to be purchased for the job.

## Lesson 3 Test Your WRC Skills (pages 46–47)

**1. D. 160**
Option D is correct because you multiplied the number of bottles per box by the number of boxes. Option A is incorrect because you divided the number of bottles per box by the number of boxes. You needed to multiply. Option B is incorrect because you subtracted 8 from 20 rather than multiplying. Option C is incorrect because you added the number of boxes to the number of bottles per box instead of multiplying.

**2. D. $23.45**
Option D is correct because you correctly multiplied the number of screws and hooks by the cost for each item to find the total costs for screws and hooks. Then you added those costs to the cost of the hammer. Option A is incorrect because you added the cost of only one screw, one hammer, and one hook. Option B is not correct because you added all the numbers in the problem together. Option C is incorrect because you multiplied all the numbers together and rounded to the nearest hundredth or cent.

**3. A. $35.45**
Option A is correct because you needed to multiply the number of each item purchased by its cost and then add the costs together. Option B is incorrect because you replaced the cost of one map with the cost of a paperback. Option C is not correct because you multiplied all of the numbers together instead of multipying, then adding. Option D is incorrect because you only found the cost of one of each item.

**4. B. 25**
Option B is correct because to find the number of cases you need to buy, you needed to divide the number of people attending by the number of bottles in each case. Option A is incorrect because it assumes that you are buying a case of water for each person (you multiplied the number of bottles in a case by the number of people attending). Option C is incorrect because you added the number of bottles in a case to the number of people who will be attending. Option D is incorrect because you subtracted the number of bottles in a case of water from the number of people who will be attending.

**5. D. $855.00**
Option D is correct. You found what you earned for the first 40 hours of work at your regular hourly rate, and then added that to the amount you made for the 5 hours of overtime that you worked. Option A is incorrect because you did not take into account the 5 hours of overtime pay. Option B is incorrect because you added $1\frac{1}{2}$ to the amount you would make if you were paid $18.00 for all your hours worked. Option C is not correct because you did not take the increased rate for the overtime hours into account—you multiplied 45 by $18.00.

**6. B. $800**
Option B is correct because you multiplied your earnings per pair of shoes sold by the number sold and then added the bonus. Option A is incorrect because you did not add the bonus. Option C is not correct because you added the number of pairs of shoes you need to sell, the amount you earn for each pair sold, and the bonus. Option D is not correct because you subtracted the bonus instead of adding it.

**7. C. 3.75 hr**
Option C is correct because you divided the number of miles traveled by the rate at which you traveled to find the time it would take you to reach the plant. Option A is incorrect because the decimal point was not placed in the correct place. Options B and D are incorrect because you did not use the correct operation (division) or apply the correct formula (distance = rate × time) to find the answer.

# Lesson 4 Test Your WRC Skills (pages 54–55)

## 1. C. $81
Option C is correct because you multiplied the number of hours you work by your wages per hour and added that to the product of the number of crates you loaded times $3.00. Option A is incorrect because you subtracted what you earned from loading crates from your earnings from hourly wages instead of adding the two totals together. Option B is incorrect because you did not add the money earned from loading crates to your hourly earnings. Option D is incorrect because you multiplied the total that you earned from hourly wages by $3.00.

## 2. B. 2,900 lb
Option B is correct because you multiplied the weight of each box by the number of boxes with that weight and then added the products together. Option A is incorrect because you only added the weight of one of each of the boxes together. Option C is incorrect because you subtracted the total weight of the boxes from the capacity of the forklift. Option D is incorrect because you calculated incorrectly.

## 3. D. $5,665
Option D is correct because you added all forms of payment and subtracted the cash that was originally in the drawer from the total. Option A is incorrect because you did not subtract the $125 that was originally in the drawer. Option B is incorrect because you added the $125 that was originally in the drawer instead of subtracting it from the total. Option C is incorrect because you did not add in the amount of the checks.

## 4. B. 14
Option B is correct because you divided both 8 and 10 by 1.25 and then added the result. Option A is incorrect because you subtracted 8 from 10. Option C is incorrect because you added the lengths of the boards together. Option D is incorrect because you multiplied the number of pieces from each board instead of adding.

## 5. A. 68
Option A is correct. To find the number of chips you assembled, you multiplied the number of chips per day by the number of days. Since you assembled 7 fewer chips this week, you subtracted 7 from the product. Option B is incorrect because you did not subtract after multiplying. Option C is incorrect because you added after the multiplication step rather than subtracting. Option D is incorrect because you multiplied 15 by 7 and then subtracted 5.

## 6. C. 31
Option C is correct because you subtracted $580 from $1,200 and then divided the difference by 20 to determine the number of sales he needs to make. Option A is incorrect because you added the number of sales he has already made to the number of sales he must make each month. Option B is incorrect because it is the total sales he must make in the month to be considered as Employee of the Month—it does not account for the $580 in sales he has already made. Option D is incorrect because it is the amount he earns in commission per sale.

## 7. B. $475
Option B is correct. You first subtracted $250 from $5,000 to find the amount that remained for bonuses. Then you divided by 10 to figure out how much each employee will receive. Option A is incorrect because you calculated incorrectly. Option C is incorrect because you divided the money without deducting the cost of the party first. Option D is incorrect because you divided the total set aside for bonuses and then subtracted the cost of the party from that amount.

## Chapter 1 Assessment (pages 58–59)

### 1. C. what is in the boxes
Option C is correct because what the boxes contain is irrelevant to the question. Option A is incorrect because knowing the weight of the boxes is essential to finding the total weight. Option B is incorrect because you need to know how many boxes there are in order to find the total weight. Option D is incorrect because you need to know what unit of weight is being used to answer the question correct.

### 2. D. $12,600
Option D is correct because you multiplied the cost of each desk ($420) by the number of desks ordered (30). Option A is incorrect because you divided the cost of one desk by the number of desks ordered instead of multiplying. Option B is incorrect because you subtracted 30 from $420 instead of multiplying. Option C is incorrect because you added 30 to $420. In this problem, you needed to multiply.

### 3. A. 1,200 ÷ 80
Option A is correct. In order to find the number of people you can register for the seminar, you need to divide the total amount budgeted ($1,200) by the registration fee per person ($80). Option B is incorrect. You have chosen the right operation but the wrong order of numbers. Option C is incorrect because subtraction is not the right operation in this situation. Option D is incorrect because multiplication is not the right operation in this situation.

### 4. C. $360
Option C is correct because you figured out the money you made for mileage and for each car towed and then you added the amounts together. Option A is incorrect because you only accounted for the cars you towed. Option B is incorrect because you only figured out what you earned for the miles you drove. Option D is incorrect because you multiplied the number of cars by the number of miles.

### 5. C. how many patients you are caring for
Option C is correct. In order for you to find the time you need to spend with each patient, you must know how many patients you are caring for. Option A is incorrect because it does not matter in this scenario what room the patient is located in. Option B is incorrect because the question does not state that the condition of the patient determines the time you spend with them. Option D is incorrect because doctors are not a factor in what your job requires of you. The number of doctors will not help you answer the question.

### 6. A. 20
Option A is correct because if you can only make 30 salads then you must subtract 50 − 30 to find the number that needs to be made to keep up with the restaurant's orders. Option B is incorrect because that represents the number you can make, not the difference between orders placed and the number you can make. Option C is incorrect because this number is irrelevant to any information presented in the problem. Option D is incorrect because you added the numbers in the problem instead of finding the difference.

### 7. B. $\frac{330}{6}$
Option B is correct because it represents how you would find the speed or rate using the formula $d = rt$. You substituted 330 for $d$ and 6 for $r$ and then solved for $t$. Option A is incorrect because multiplying would result in 1,980, which would be an unreasonable answer. Option C is incorrect because subtraction is not used to find the speed you must travel. Option D is incorrect because addition is not used to find the speed you must travel.

### 8. C. 640
Option C is correct because you multiplied the number of bags in each type of box by the number of each type of box you packed and then added the products together. Option A is incorrect because you found the total number of boxes packed and did not account for how many bags are in each type of box. Option B is incorrect because you added all of the numbers in the problem together. Option D is incorrect because you multiplied all of the numbers in the problem together.

## Lesson 5 Test Your WRC Skills (pages 68–69)

**1. C. $157.00**

Option C is correct because you lined the decimals up and added correctly. Option A is incorrect because you inserted the decimal point as you would if you had multiplied instead of added. Option B is incorrect because you forgot to include the cost of the file folders. Option D is incorrect because you added all of the amounts as if they were whole numbers.

**2. C. $145.50**

Option C is correct because you multiplied your hourly rate by the number of hours you work in one day. Option A is incorrect because it is the amount you earn each hour. Option B is incorrect because you multiplied your hourly wage by the number of days you work in one week, not the number of hours in one day. Option D is incorrect. This is the amount you earn in a week.

**3. B. $10.47**

Option B is correct because you added the cost of the correct items and lined up the decimal points. Option A is incorrect because you did not include the cost of the fruit smoothie. Option C is incorrect because you added the cost of a juice instead of a coffee. Option D is incorrect because you added the cost of all of the items, not just the items ordered.

**4. D. $1,594.90**

Option D is correct because you multiplied the amount made on the sale of one phone and one accessories package by the number of sales of each item and then added the products together to find the total sales. Option A is incorrect because you found the amount of money made by the sale of only one phone and one accessories package. Option B is incorrect because it is only the amount of sales you made from phones. It does not include the sales from the accessories packages. Option C is incorrect. Instead of adding the amount from the total sales of the phones and the accessories packages, you subtracted the amount of sales from the accessories packages from the amount of sales from the phones.

**5. A. two quarters, one dime, one nickel, and one penny**

Option A is correct. This represents $0.66 in change. Option B is incorrect because you subtracted $10.00 − $9.34 incorrectly; you are giving the customer $0.76 in change. Options C and D are both incorrect because each option includes too many quarters for the correct change.

**6. A. $32.03**

Option A is correct because you added all of the money you have spent so far and then subtracted that total from $450.00. Option B is incorrect because you did not subtract the cost of the hotel. Option C is incorrect. This is your expense total so far. Option D is incorrect. You added the amount budgeted for travel expenses to your expenses so far.

**7. D. one dollar, two dimes, and four pennies**

Option D is correct. The correct amount of change that you should receive is $1.24. Options A and B are incorrect because each option includes 2 dollars, which would mean that the bill was less than $123.00. The actual bill is greater than $123.00. Option C is incorrect. This would be the correct change if the bill were $123.74.

## Lesson 6 Test Your WRC Skills (pages 76–77)

**1. C. 12%**

Option C is correct because you divided $6 by $50 to find the answer. Once you completed the division, you changed the answer to a percent by moving the decimal point two places to the right. Option A is incorrect because you forgot to move the decimal point two places to the right when changing to a percent. Option B is incorrect because you used the amount of the commission as the percent. Option D is incorrect because you moved the decimal point too many places.

**2. A. 12.5%**

Option A is correct because you divided the amount spent on decorations by the total amount spent on the luncheon, then converted the answer to a percent. Option B is incorrect. This represents the percent spent on the room rental fee, not the decorations. Option C is incorrect because you used the amount of money spent (the part) as the percent. Option D is incorrect because this represents the percent of the money spent on food.

**3. B. $32.50**

Option B is correct because you changed the percent to a decimal (or fraction) and multiplied $0.05 \times \$650$. Option A is incorrect because you used the percent as the amount that she pays each week (the part). Option B is incorrect because you did not place the decimal point properly. Option D is incorrect. You found the amount of Gretchen's check that does not go towards health insurance.

**4. C. 15%**

Option C is correct. To find the percent, you divided the part ($1,500) by the whole ($10,000) and then converted the answer to a percent. Option A is incorrect because you did not change the decimal to a percent after dividing. Option B is incorrect because you did not place the decimal point properly. Option D is incorrect. The answer is not reasonable because the sales of the lawn and garden department would have to be higher than the total sales for the entire store, which is impossible.

**5. D. 62.5%**

Option D is correct. A key word in this problem is NOT. To find the percent of calories NOT from fat, first you subtracted 210 from 560 to get 350. Then you divided 350 by 560 and converted the answer to a percent. Option A is incorrect because you misplaced the decimal point and you found the percent of total calories from fat. Option B is incorrect because you misplaced the decimal point. Option C is incorrect because you found the percent of total calories from fat.

**6. B. 38.5%**

Option B is correct. You found the total sales from the two categories ($693) and then found the total sales of all the categories ($1,800). To find the percent, you divided $693 by $1,800 and then converted the answer to a percent. Option A is incorrect because you did not convert to a percent. Option C is incorrect. You added the amounts for the sales of decorations and the collectibles instead of the candles and gift cards. Option D is incorrect because you divided the whole by the part, converted to a percent, and then rounded.

## Chapter 2 Assessment (pages 80–81)

**1. C. $510**

Option C is correct because you found the amount that was 20% of his paycheck and multiplied that amount by 3. Option A is incorrect. This is the amount he deposited from each paycheck. Option B is incorrect because it is the amount deposited after 2 paychecks. Option D is incorrect. This is the amount he would have deposited if he were paid every week ($170 × 6), but the problem states that he is paid every 2 weeks.

**2. B. $3.51**

Option B is correct. You added the cost of the two items, multiplied by 10% to find the amount of the discount, and then subtracted the amount of the discount. Option A is incorrect. This is the amount of discount only. Option C is incorrect. You found the total cost of the two items at their original price—you did not subtract the amount of the discount. Option D is incorrect. You found the total cost of the items and then added the amount of the 10% discount instead of subtracting.

**3. D. $492.00**

Option D is correct because you multiplied the hourly wage, the number of hours worked each day, and number of days worked together. Option A is incorrect. This is the amount Beth earns in one hour. Option B is incorrect. This is the amount she earns after 8 hours, or 1 day. Option C is incorrect. This is the amount she earned after working 5 days, but she worked 6 days in the week, not 5.

**4. A. $84.05**

Option A is correct because you subtracted both costs from the maintenance budget. Option B is incorrect because you only subtracted the expense of cleaning and waxing the floors. Option C is incorrect because you only subtracted the cost of fixing the air conditioning. Option D is incorrect because instead of subtracting from the budgeted amount, you added the expenses to it.

**5. C. 10**

Option C is correct. You found 20% of the number of patients on each floor and added those numbers together to find the total. Option A is incorrect because you only found 20% of the patients on the third floor. Option B is incorrect because you only found 20% of the patients on the fourth floor. Option D is incorrect because it is the total number of patients on both floors.

**6. B. $2,056.04**

Option B is correct. You divided his total earnings for 6 months by 6 to find his earnings for 1 month. Option A is incorrect because you divided his earnings for 6 months by 12 instead of 6. Option C is incorrect because you divided his earnings for 6 months by 3 when you should have divided by 6. Option D is incorrect because you multiplied by 6 instead of dividing.

**7. C. $63.99**

Option C is correct because you added the cost of the two additional services to the standard cable cost. Option A is incorrect because you subtracted the price of the two services from the cost of the standard package rather than adding them to it. Option B is incorrect because you did not add the cost of the two extra services to find the total cost. Option D is incorrect. You added the cost of all the extra services available to the cost of the standard package when the problem stated that you only added two of the services.

## Lesson 7 Test Your WRC Skills (pages 90–91)

**1. C. feet**

Option C is correct. Using feet would be the most logical unit of measure to use when measuring the dimensions of a deck. Option A is incorrect. Although yards are a unit used to measure length, they would not be used because they would not give you the level of precision needed. Option B is incorrect because gallons are a unit of liquid measurement. Option D is incorrect because tons are used to measure weight, not length.

**2. D. scale**

Option D is correct because a scale is the only option that measures weight. Options A and B are incorrect because both a ruler and a yardstick are tools that measure the length of an object. Option C is incorrect because it measures capacity, not weight.

**3. A. ounces**

Option A is correct because they are the most precise unit of weight. Option B is incorrect because although tons are a unit of weight, they are much too large to be used when measuring ingredients for a cake. Option C is incorrect because inches are used to measure length. Option D is incorrect because a gallon is a measure of capacity, or liquid measure, not weight.

**4. A. inches**

Option A is correct because most picture frames are measured in inches. Options B and C are incorrect because feet and yards are generally too large for a frame measurement, especially one with the measures given in the problem. Option D is incorrect. A gallon is a unit of liquid measure, not linear measure.

**5. D. miles**

Option D is correct. Miles are the appropriate unit of measurement for measuring distances that a truck driver would travel. Option A is incorrect because feet are too small a unit of measure to use when tracking driving distance. Option B is incorrect. Although bigger than feet, this unit of measurement is still too small. Option C is incorrect because tons measure weight, not length (distance).

**6. D. $\frac{3}{4}$ in.**

Option D is correct because inches measure length and are the most reasonable unit to measure an object of that size. Options A and B are incorrect. Feet and yards are both too large to measure something like a nail. Option C is incorrect. Pounds are used to measure weight, not length.

**7. B. 5 lb**

Option B is correct. 5 pounds would be the most appropriate weight for a brick. Option A is incorrect. Ounces are used to measure weight, but 5 ounces is not a reasonable weight for a brick. Option C is incorrect. One ton is equal to 2,000 pounds, so 5 tons is very heavy and is far more than a single brick would weigh. Option D is incorrect because gallons are a measure of capacity, not weight.

**8. A. tape measure**

Option A is correct because a tape measure is used to find linear dimensions, such as the measurements of a room. Option B is incorrect because a protractor is used in geometry to find the measure of an angle. Option C is incorrect because a measuring cup is used to measure capacity, not length. Option D is incorrect. A compass is not used to measure length.

## Lesson 8 Test Your WRC Skills (pages 98–99)

**1. B. 60 pieces**
Option B is correct because you converted 6 feet to 2 yards and divided the length of the football field by 2. Option A is incorrect because you divided 120 yards by 6 feet, so you did not convert feet to yards first. Option C is incorrect. This is the length of the field in yards. Option D is incorrect. This is the length of the field in feet.

**2. C. 4 c**
Option C is correct because you are doubling the recipe, so there are 2 pints of buttermilk required. You correctly converted 2 pints to 4 cups. Option A is incorrect. You chose the capacity of your measuring cup, or you divided when converting instead of multiplying. Remember that when going from larger units to smaller units, you need to multiply. Option B is incorrect because you forgot to double the recipe. Option D is incorrect because this represents the amount of buttermilk if you had quadrupled the recipe (or needed to use 4 pints).

**3. B. 1.25 lb**
Option B is correct. You correctly converted from ounces to pounds by dividing 20 ounces by 16 because there are 16 ounces in 1 pound. Option A is incorrect because 20 ounces is greater than 1 pound. Option C is incorrect. You needed to convert from ounces to pounds, but instead you subtracted the 16 ounces from the 20 ounces. Option D is incorrect because you multiplied 20 ounces by 16 ounces instead of dividing.

**4. B. $1\frac{1}{3}$ ft by $1\frac{2}{3}$ ft**
Option B is correct. You must convert inches to feet, so you divided each dimension by 12. Options A and C are incorrect because you used an incorrect equivalent measure to convert. There are 12 inches in 1 foot. Option D is incorrect because you multiplied each dimension by 12 instead of dividing by 12.

**5. D. 2 gal**
Option D is correct. You needed to find the number of cups of olive oil you needed each day, then multiply that by 7 days, and then convert that to gallons. Since you needed just over 1 gallon for the week, you needed to tell the chef to order 2 gallons. Option A is incorrect because you multiplied by 16 instead of dividing. Options B and C are incorrect because you gave an amount that you would need for less than one week. You will not have enough for the seventh day if you only have 1 gallon or less.

**6. B. 2.25 lb**
Option B is correct. You are converting from smaller units to larger units, so you divided 36 ounces by 16 to find the number of pounds. Option A is incorrect. There are 16 ounces in a pound, not 36. Option C is incorrect; you did not use the correct equivalent units when you divided. Option D is incorrect because you multiplied the equivalent units rather than dividing.

**7. C. 4 qt**
Option C is correct. There are 4 cups in 1 quart. Since you are converting from a smaller unit to a larger unit, you divide 16 by 4. Option A is incorrect because there are not 16 cups in 1 quart. Option B is incorrect because you used an incorrect equivalent measure when converting. Option D is incorrect because you multiplied the units instead of dividing.

## Lesson 9 Test Your WRC Skills (pages 106–107)

### 1. B. 50 mph
Option B is correct. You used the formula $D = r \times t$ and divided the distance you needed to travel by the time. Option A is incorrect because this is the time you have rather than the rate of speed you must travel. Option C is incorrect. You entered one of the values into the equation incorrectly or did not calculate correctly. Option D is incorrect. You multiplied instead of divided. This speed is not reasonable.

### 2. D. 240 sq. ft
Option D is correct because you needed to find the area of the room, so you used the formula $A = l \times w$ and multiplied the length of the room by the width. Option A is incorrect because you added the two measures rather than multiplying them. Option B is incorrect. You multiplied the width of the laminate by the width of the room. Option C is incorrect because you multiplied the width of the laminate by the length of the room. The width of the laminate is irrelevant.

### 3. C. $V = l \times w \times h$
Option C is correct because this is the formula you would use to find volume of the aquarium. Option A is incorrect because this is the distance formula. Option B is incorrect. This is the formula you would use to find the area of a rectangle. Option D is incorrect. This is the formula you would use to find the perimeter of a rectangle.

### 4. B. 180 yd
Option B is correct. Finding the amount of fencing needed means finding the perimeter of the space that needs to be fenced. Option A is incorrect because you only added two of the four sides of the fence. Add all four sides to find the perimeter. Option C is incorrect. You found the area of the space rather than finding the perimeter. Option D is incorrect. You found the volume of the space. The measure of 1.5 yards is irrelevant to the question.

### 5. A. 36 min
Option A is correct because you used the formula $D = r \times t$. You also correctly converted the units from a decimal part of 1 hour to the correct number of minutes. Option B is incorrect because you added the two numbers together instead of using the formula $D = r \times t$. Option C is incorrect. It is the same as Option B converted to hours and minutes. Option D is incorrect because you subtracted the speed from the distance in miles rather than applying the distance formula. This answer is not reasonable for the situation.

### 6. C. 180 ft
Option C is correct. You added the length of all the sides of the store to find the perimeter. Option A is incorrect because you only accounted for the one wall you measured, when the store has four walls. You need enough for all four walls. Option B is incorrect because you added only two sides of the store. Option D is incorrect because you used the formula for area instead of perimeter.

### 7. A. Sandbox 1
Option A is correct. It has an area of 144 square feet, which is the largest area of all of the sandboxes. Option B is incorrect because the area is 140 square feet. There is a larger sandbox available. Option C is incorrect. The area is only 128 square feet. There are other sandboxes that are larger. Option D is incorrect. This is the sandbox with the smallest area.

## Chapter 3 Assessment (pages 110–111)

**1. B. 4 yd**
Option B is correct because there are 3 feet in 1 yard and $12 \div 3 = 4$. Option A is incorrect because you divided by 4 instead of 3. There are 3 feet in 1 yard. Option C is incorrect because instead of dividing by 3, you divided by 2. Option D is incorrect because you multiplied by 3 instead of dividing.

**2. A. scale**
Option A is correct because a scale is used to measure dry ingredients in units such as ounces or pounds. Options B and C are incorrect because a ruler and a tape measure are used to measure length. Option D is incorrect because a tablespoon measures units that are too small to be appropriate for this situation.

**3. C. $26.10**
Option C is correct. You used the area formula to find the square footage (area) of the room to be cleaned and then multiplied the area by $0.15. Option A is incorrect because you placed your decimal point in the wrong place. Option B is incorrect. You multiplied the price per square foot by the perimeter of the room instead of the area. Option D is incorrect because it is the area of the room. You need to multiply the area by the price per square foot to find the cost to the customer.

**4. A. 4 c**
Option A is correct because you divided 32 by 8 and the result is 4. Option B is incorrect because you subtracted 8 from 32 instead of dividing. Option C is incorrect because you multiplied the 32 ounces by the price of the soft drink. The price is irrelevant to the question. Option D is incorrect because you multiplied 32 by 8 instead of dividing.

**5. D. Aquarium 4**
Option D is correct. Aquarium 4 has a volume of 2,000 cubic inches. You multiplied all of the dimensions to find the volume. Option A is incorrect. This represents the aquarium with the smallest volume. Option B is incorrect. It has a volume of 1,728 cubic inches and there is another aquarium with a greater volume. Option C is incorrect. It has a volume of 1,680 cubic inches, which is not the greatest volume.

**6. D. 80 in.**
Option D is correct because you multiplied 6 feet by 12 and then added the remaining 8 inches. Option A is incorrect because you added the feet and the inches together without converting the feet to inches first. Option B is incorrect. You multiplied the feet by the inches rather than converting the feet to inches and then adding. Option C is incorrect. You correctly converted 6 feet to inches but did not add the remaining 8 inches.

**7. B. feet**
Option B is correct. Feet would be the most logical unit of measurement to use. Option A is incorrect. Inches are too small a unit for this situation. Option C is incorrect because pounds measure weight, not length. Option D is incorrect because gallons are used for measuring capacity rather than length.

## Lesson 10 Test Your WRC Skills (pages 120–121)

**1. C. 8**
Option C is correct because the mode of a data set is the value that appears the greatest number of times. The home team scored 8 runs in three games. The other options are incorrect because each value is the number of runs scored in only two games.

**2. B. Add the prices together and divide by seven.**
Option B is correct because it describes how to determine the mean from a data set of 7 values. Option A is incorrect because it divides by the mode rather than the number of values in the data set. Option C is not correct because it describes how to find the median. Option D is incorrect because it describes how to find the range.

**3. A. the price of the most expensive donut**
Option A is correct because the range is the difference between the least and greatest values of a data set. Option B is incorrect because the price of the customers' favorite donut may or may not be the most expensive donut that the bakery sells. Option C and D are not correct because the range of the donuts' prices does not depend on the number sold.

**4. B. $22**
Option B is correct because the median is the "middle value" in a data set. The other options are incorrect because they are not the middle value. Option D is the range of the customers' spending, not the median.

**5. B. 182 lb**
Option B is correct. You calculated the mean weight by finding the sum of the measurements of weight, then you divided by the total number of measurements, which is 8. The other options are incorrect because they are either less or greater than the mean weight.

**6. D. 6.0 hours**
Option D is correct. If three values have a mean of 4.0 and two of the values are 3.0, then the third value must be greater than 4.0. To check Option D, you found the sum of 6.0, 3.0, and 3.0, which is 12.0. Then you divided by 3 to find the mean of 4.0. The other options are incorrect because each would provide a mean running time for the battery that is less than 4.0 hours.

**7. C. List the ratings in order from least to greatest, and select the fourth rating.**
Option C is correct because the fourth value in a set of seven is the "middle," or median value. Option A is incorrect because it describes the mean, not the median. Option B is incorrect because it identifies the "middle day" of the week, not the middle value of the ratings. Option D describes the mode, not the median.

**8. B. At least one of the other workers earns less than $10.50 per hour.**
Option B is correct. If you earn more than the mean among a group of employees, then someone else must earn less than the mean. Option A is incorrect because it is possible that the mean is not a value in the data set. Option C is incorrect because you might be the only employee that earns more than the mean. Option D is incorrect because several workers could earn the same pay.

## Lesson 11 Test Your WRC Skills (pages 128–129)

### 1. C. (Rate × Miles) + Tolls

Option C is correct because it applies to every row in the table. Note that the rate is given in units of dollars per mile, such as $2.40/mile or $2.80/mile. This means that a trip of 10 miles would cost either $24.00 or $28.00, plus tolls. Option A is incorrect because adding the mileage to the tolls does not accurately represent the amount to be charged. Option B is incorrect because you added the miles to the tolls and then multiplied by the rate, but you should not multiply the amount for tolls by the rate. Option D is incorrect because rate and miles must be multiplied together, not divided.

### 2. B. $146.00

Option B is correct because it is the sum of $84.00 and $62.00, which are the two charges for Cole Accounting. Options A and C are incorrect because Cole Accounting had two trips with the driver, not just one. Option D is incorrect because it identifies a charge for another customer.

### 3. A. $19.60

Option A is correct. To solve, you calculated the per mile savings to be $2.80/mile − $2.40/mile = $0.40/mile. The trip on 3/13 was 49 miles, so the savings is 49 miles × $0.40/mile = $19.60. Option B is incorrect because it assumed the customer saves money on tolls. Option C is incorrect because it used data that does not apply to 3/13. Option D is incorrect because it is the cost of the trip, not the savings.

### 4. B. Train 6

Option B is correct because Train 6 takes 50 minutes for the trip. The other options are incorrect because Train 34 takes 1 hour and Train 29 takes 55 minutes. Train 14 does not travel to Regina Station.

### 5. A. 5:40 P.M.

Option A is correct. Train 6 arrives at Kiernan Station at 6:20 P.M., and it departs 18th Street at 5:55 P.M. Fifteen minutes before 5:55 P.M. is 5:40 P.M. Option B is incorrect because you would arrive at 18th Street Station at 6:00 P.M. and miss Train 6. Option C is incorrect because it applies to Train 34, which arrives Kiernan Station at 6:01 P.M. Option D is incorrect because it applies to Train 34 and the Downtown Station.

### 6. D. 1 package from Maryland Scientific

Option D is correct. Its cost of $76.50 is the lowest cost for a set of 90 slides. Option A has a cost of $78.00. Option B has a cost of $79.20. Option C has a cost of $81.60.

## Lesson 12 Test Your WRC Skills (pages 136–137)

**1. D. Value**
Option D is correct because the ratings for value are widely spread from 2 to 9. The other options are incorrect because the data in each of the other columns is concentrated within a narrower range.

**2. D. Service ratings are unrelated to the size of the party.**
Option D is correct because the ratings for service fall within a narrow range, and the ratings do not form a pattern with the data for size of party. The other options are incorrect because they suggest a relationship that the data does not show. Option C is not correct because the data provides no information about families and children at the restaurant.

**3. A. giving the survey to many customers over one week**
Option A is correct. As a general rule, increasing the number of participants and the variety of participants increases the reliability of a survey. Option B is incorrect because it does not increase the representation of the restaurants' customers. Options C and D are incorrect because each distorts the data in favor of the restaurant.

**4. C. Of the 20 responses, 3 were from the same customer.**
Option C is correct because the same customer would be counted 3 times in the survey. Option A is incorrect because it is a fact about the customers, not the survey that represents them. Option B is incorrect because randomly choosing participants helps make a survey reliable. Option D is incorrect because first-time customers may be a part of the parking lot's customer base.

**5. A. The lot will lose about $\frac{1}{3}$ of its daily customers.**
Option A is correct. According to the survey, about 20% of the customers will switch to a new lot. About 30% of the customers will become half-time customers, which is a loss of about 15%. These percentages add to a loss of 35%, which is close to $\frac{1}{3}$. Option B is incorrect because the loss is closer to $\frac{1}{3}$ than to $\frac{1}{2}$. Option C is incorrect because the data do not suggest a gain in customers. Option D is incorrect because it presents a specific range of customers. The data do not indicate the number of customers of the parking lot, only the number of customers surveyed.

**6. B. $\frac{1}{4}$**
Option B is correct because 25 out of 100 people is the same as a probability of 25%, or $\frac{25}{100}$, which equals $\frac{1}{4}$. The other options are incorrect because they do not equal this fraction.

## Chapter 4 Assessment (pages 140–141)

### 1. A. 41.0 cm
Option A is correct. You found the mean by adding the values of length together, then dividing the sum by the number of values. The other options are incorrect because they represent incorrect calculations of the mean.

### 2. D. median and mode
Option D is correct. The median is the value that falls in the middle of a data set, and the mode is the value that appears most often in the set. Option A is incorrect because the range is the difference between the least and greatest values of the data set, which here is $0.25. Options B and C are incorrect because the mean of this data set is less than $5.80.

### 3. A. Fran's Gourmet Dog Food
Option A is correct. Among the brands without fish, Fran's Gourmet Dog Food has the lowest price. To find the price per pound, you divided the total cost by the number of pounds: $\frac{\$61.20}{30} = \$2.04$ per pound. Options B and D are incorrect because they have higher prices per pound. Option C is incorrect because this dog food contains fish, which the customer does not want.

### 4. C. $130.00
Option C is correct. First you calculated the price of four 1-day tickets for the family: $4 \times (\$50.00 + \$50.00 + \$20.00 + \$30.00) = \$600.00$. Then you subtracted the value of 4-day tickets for the family: $160.00 + $160.00 + $60.00 + $90.00 = $470.00. Finally, you subtracted: $600.00 – $470.00 = $170.00. The other options are incorrect because they do not correctly calculate the two prices or their difference.

### 5. D. Give the survey to many more customers.
Option D is correct because a sample of five customers might not represent all the customers accurately. Surveying more customers would help show whether or not the rating of 2 in the data set was an outlier or a true reflection of customers' opinions. Option A is incorrect. This option would be reasonable if you knew that the rating of 2 was unreliable, making it an outlier. But with such a small set of data this rating could be legitimate. Option B is incorrect because it deliberately misrepresents the data. Option C is incorrect because the five customers may or may not have experiences that represent all of the customers.

### 6. B. $\frac{1}{5}$
Option B is correct. Of the total number of orders in 1 hour, $\frac{4}{20}$ or $\frac{1}{5}$ of those orders were for strawberry ice cream. So $\frac{1}{5}$ is the probability that a randomly-chosen customer will order strawberry. Option A is incorrect because it is the probability of choosing 1 of 7 flavors that were equal in popularity. Strawberry is more popular than most of the flavors, as the data table shows. Option C is incorrect because the number of total orders (20) was incorrectly reduced to 7 when it should be 5. Option D is incorrect because the probability of any event is always equal to or between 0 and 1.